God Hates Abuse

GOD HATES ABUSE

Abuse and the Doctrine of Headship and Submission

ROBIN MULLINS SENGER

Copyright © 2019 by Robin Mullins Senger

All rights reserved. This book may be freely shared and quoted from as long as credit is given to the author and a link provided to www.godhatesabuse.org.

Printed in the United States of America
First Printing, 2016

CreateSpace
ISBN-13: 978-1983543197
ISBN-10: 1983543195

Ingram
ISBN-13: 978-0578472706

God Hates Abuse Project
PO Box 273042
Fort Collins, CO 80527

www.godhatesabuse.org

All Scripture quotations, unless otherwise indicated, are taken from The Holy Bible, New Revised Standard Version Bible, copyright © 1989 the Division of Christian Education of the National Council of the Churches of Christ in the United States of America. Scripture quotations marked (AMP) are taken from the Amplified Bible, copyright © 1987 Scriptures marked (NASB) are taken from the New American Standard Bible, Copyright © 1995 by The Lockman Foundation. Scriptures marked (TPT) are taken from The Passion Translation®. Copyright © 2017 by BroadStreet Publishing® Group, LLC. Used by permission. All rights reserved.

Cover design by SelfPubBookCovers.com/BeeJavier

This book provides limited information on faith, domestic violence and relevant stories from my life. I tried to be as accurate as possible. Conversations and recollections come from my perspective and memory. I retold them in a way that evokes the feeling and meaning. In all instances, the essence of dialog is accurate.
I do not offer legal or other professional advice. I shall have no liability or responsibility regarding any loss or damage incurred, or alleged to have incurred, by the information in this book. Please seek expertise for your personal situation from professionals such as law enforcement, legal counsel, therapists, safe houses, advocacy and other services. Readers should take full responsibility for their safety and know their limits.
Resources are for informational purposes only. I do not necessarily endorse all information, products or services provided by them. Links are subject to change, expire or redirect with no notice.

For my Sky-Bird, my Joy-Bird, and my Song-Bird, who inspire me every day to live free, dance silly and sing loud. For my husband and best friend Kyle, who helped me become who I wanted and needed to be. May we never stop laughing together!

Most of all, I dedicate this to God, who gave me hope in the promise of Isaiah 51:3 after I fled. He extravagantly fulfilled every word. Truly Lord, You turned my wilderness into a lovely garden and filled it to overflowing with joy, gladness, thanksgiving and songs of praise to You!

Contents

Acknowledgment ix
Chapter 1: The Crisis That Birthed This Book 1
Chapter 2: How to Use the "Reflection" Section 5
Chapter 3: A Dangerous Mistake 9
Chapter 4: The Crossroads of Redemption 17
Chapter 5: Abusive or Ignorant? 27
Chapter 6: Isolation Is Dangerous 37
Chapter 7: Where Is Your Marriage on This Scale? 43
Chapter 8: Is His Fruit Good or Toxic? 51
Chapter 9: Don't You Dare Judge Me! 63
Chapter 10: How to Interpret Scripture 73
Chapter 11: Headship and Submission 87
Chapter 12: Escaping the Ultimate Loneliness 115
Chapter 13: Options 147
Chapter 14: A Biblical Response to Abuse 179
Chapter 15: Grief and Forgiveness 201
Chapter 16: Freedom from Fear 215
Appendix A: Chronic Personality Problems 229
Appendix B: 21 Signs of an Abusive Parent 233
Appendix C: Risk Assessment 237
Appendix D: Safety Plan 241
Appendix E: Technology Safety Plan 247

Appendix F: Pet Safety and Custody. 253
Appendix G: Scripture for Prayer and Meditation 257
Exercise A: What Are Your Values? 267
Exercise B: Draw Out Your Gremlin 269
Exercise C: Calm the "Monkey Mind" 271
Exercise D: Detox Your Toxic Relationships 273
Exercise E: No More Excuses 281
Exercise F: How Is Your Self-Care? 285
Exercise G: Daily Self-Care Guide 289
Resources 291
Works Cited. 299
About the Author. 305

Acknowledgment

This book would not be possible without those special people willing to walk with me at a time of personal risk and the inevitable messiness that accompanies domestic abuse.

The primary weapon abusers use is isolation and secrecy. I will never forget the first time I reached out for help. I didn't tell the person everything. I wanted to see what the reaction would be to a little of what was happening and if he thought I was as crazy as I felt. The response was compassionate and emboldened me to speak up more. With the support of a half-dozen people, I gained the courage and strength to flee. At our new home, I encountered more people brave enough to walk with me through divorce and recovery.

For the privacy of these people, I will not list their names here, but they know who they are. I will always be thankful to them for picking me up when I fell down, believing in me when I didn't believe in myself, and inspiring me to be more than I ever dreamed I could be. Some of them were in my life briefly, but I will never forget their kindness. A few of them have been with me for the long haul and have proven to be true friends and mentors of tremendous value and worth. I love them dearly!

Credentials

I want to make clear up front I am not a theologian, counselor or psychologist and do not pretend to be. I bring years of experience from the trenches of my toxic and abusive relationships and helping others through theirs. I value my experience as an advocate and serve faith-based victims and survivors through my non-profit *God Hates Abuse Project*. You can learn more at www.godhatesabuse.org.

Rather than offer my own biblical interpretations, this book leans on the expertise of trained pastors and other religious leaders. What I learned from them helped me in making sense of what I had experienced, and I share it in hopes it will help you too. For brevity, I only quote what I feel is most useful in a crisis when there is not time or freedom for deeper research. Get the books, visit the websites, and delve deeper into the authors work as you can.

In this new edition, I have added life-coaching questions and tips for gaining traction in a particular subject, such as making difficult decisions or developing boundaries. I love helping victims and survivors conquer the debilitating victim mentality, move beyond a pattern of toxic relationships, and live a fulfilling life. As a Toxic Relationship Resilience Life Coach, I will ask you questions so you can get unstuck and increase the likelihood of moving forward successfully. This will help you gain confidence and an optimistic outlook for continued growth.

Take the information I offer and decide for yourself if it's right. Ask questions. Study the referenced Scriptures for yourself. Pray about it. Do more research on it. Take the pieces you find valuable and discard the rest. But please, read with an open mind and heart, asking the Lord to speak to you through His Word and this book. I pray you find the knowledge and truth you seek!

Chapter 1

The Crisis That Birthed This Book

GOD HATES ABUSE is a book of hope for Christian wives caught in the web of spousal abuse and violence.

This book grew out of my journey of recovery and healing from a dangerous and abusive marriage. My husband, Brian (not his real name), believed God gave him the right to rule his family. It was after I fled with our children I did extensive research to find out if there was any biblical justification for my decision to leave. What I discovered shattered a spiritual paradigm of unquestioned male superiority and along with it my guilt for not "submitting" to my husband's spiritual headship.

I blogged about my journey in finding acceptance, comfort and peace from the Bible in the face of spousal abuse. Sharing my journey online was therapeutic although I expected no one to read it. However, my story resonated with many readers. They shared similar feelings of confusion over perceived biblical laws of headship and submission. None of these perceptions was compassionate toward them as victims of spiritual, emotional, economic, legal and physical abuse by their husbands.

While still in my marriage, I could not find the help I needed to resolve my spiritual conflict. Monitored, I had to be cautious of anything that might tip off Brian that I was anything less than grateful and thrilled with him. Careful to erase my history on the computer, I searched often for spiritual guidance in an abusive marriage, but only found a plethora of websites telling me to submit or burn. They added to my confusion rather than offering anything helpful. Not that I wanted a divorce. I wanted to survive my marriage with some modicum of internal peace. In the end, I fled out of desperation to protect my children.

From the safety of our new home, I delved into the spiritual implications of what I had just done. To my great surprise and relief, I learned I had not committed some unforgivable sin. I was not wicked, crazy or selfish. Best of all, I had done something that pleased God and aligned with His purpose. My relationship with God flourished and my children thrived. Even though starting over was hard, God helped us every step of the way.

This book does not condone divorce for every unhappy marriage! I am offering insight for Christian women who find themselves in a dangerous and destructive marriage and believe they have no alternative but to submit to violence and abuse.

My goal is to open a new window of thought, shift the paradigm, and start you on your own journey of self-discovery and renewed faith and hope. Where abuse has fractured your relationship with your heavenly Father, I hope to facilitate the start of spiritual healing and restoration.

Victims often struggle with deciphering between love, immaturity, ignorance and the abusive. It is confusing when there are many dynamics and emotions involved. Still, there are clear biblical guidelines to help bring clarity to each individual situation. I conformed to Brian's biblical interpretation out of fear of him and uncertainty about God's expectations.

As time went by, I often questioned my sanity and value. Reality was a mixed up, confusing and painful mess. Even though trained as a domestic violence advocate, acknowledging the signs in my marriage was difficult. My desire to please God added to the guilt and weight of it all.

As I hope to prove to you in this book, faith in God is not misplaced, and He is not condemning those who suffer the oppression of abuse. God used my marriage to Brian to teach me the truth about who He is, and what He wants for women who find themselves trapped in heart-breaking relationships. Coming into the knowledge of biblical truth allowed inner healing and personal growth that stopped the cycle of abuse. It opened the door to an amazing life full of peace and joy and being able to walk in His purpose for my life. I can say now it was all worth it. Every bit of pain and heartache was worth it to experience the life I now enjoy with my precious daughters.

Read the Bible for yourself. Take the information in this book and line it up with your own study of the Bible. 1 Thessalonians 5:21 admonishes us to *"test everything; hold fast to what is good."* Begin a private conversation with God about everything that weighs on you. Follow what He reveals to you in His Word and how He leads you. He will never fail you in this.

According to the United Nations Office on Drugs and Crime: *Global Study on Homicide, Gender-Related Killing of Women and Girls, 2018*:

> A total of 87,000 women were intentionally killed in 2017. More than half of them (58 percent) 50,000 were killed by intimate partners or family members, meaning that 137

women across the world are killed by a member of their own family every day. More than a third (30,000) of the women intentionally killed in 2017 were killed by their current or former intimate partner—someone they would normally expect to trust. (1)

Abuse to the point of death for women is so common it doesn't make the news much. Many of these statistics are Christian wives, hoping their husband would learn to love them and their children if they prayed harder and submitted more. Or that God would miraculously change him.

God has already given women ample concessions for leaving abuse, and He promises to help them through the difficulties they encounter if they will but trust Him through it. Many have left and succeeded at creating a new life of peace and fulfillment. It's difficult, but it can be done!

This book will empower Christian wives with spiritual knowledge to respond to abuse in the best way possible for them. Peace with God, combined with community resources and support, is a set-up for a better life free from abuse. Violence is NOT God's will for anyone. Victims can live free of guilt, shame and feeling like a hypocrite if they leave their abuser, or even if they stay.

I hope that God's overflowing heart of love for the oppressed and victimized is revealed in this book, and that victims will find hope, clarity and renewed faith for courageous living!

Chapter 2

How to Use the "Reflection" Section

AT THE END of each chapter are questions and tips to inspire you to reflect more on an issue brought up in the chapter. Within you is all the knowledge and wisdom you need to handle whatever it is you are facing. I want to help you access it with questions designed to draw it to the surface where it can serve you.

By understanding yourself better, you can identify what matters to YOU and what YOU want. You don't need others to decide these things for you and tell you what to think and do. It's time to take back your mind and will and step into the life you and your children deserve. You are stronger than you know!

Think about your future. As victims we often stay on a hamster wheel of rehearsing everything that is going wrong. We play the scenarios over and over in our mind. The only thing that does is reinforce a victim mentality that will keep you stuck.

If you are in a crisis, turning your attention to the future will empower you to create what you want and need to move past the crisis. The past can't be changed, but your future is a blank slate waiting for you to shape it in a way that serves you.

Use the questions and tips to create clarity and move toward the life you want. Yes, it may seem impossible, perhaps even dangerous. There are always other people and situations to consider and obstacles to overcome. In your situation it is especially difficult. But if you stay where you are, doing what you have always done, will your life be any better? What if you tried, and it DID work out?

Before you start, please have a notebook to record answers to the reflection questions, new insight, and things you want to think through more. There are benefits to writing things down rather than trusting memory. Writing things down, in addition to processing with others, helps you:

- Clear your mind
- Clarify your goals, priorities and intentions
- Reduce overwhelm
- Recognize and process your emotions
- Think outside the box and learn more
- Stay motivated
- Remember more
- Gain a sense of achievement
- Be more committed

Before continuing, reflect on the following questions to help guide you through the rest of the book. You can just pick one or two questions out of each section to work on. You do not have to answer all of them to gain benefit. Pick something that resonates with you and get started!

- If there was an outcome you secretly looked for as a result of reading this book, what would it be?
- What do you WANT in life, but don't have?
- What do you HAVE in your life, but DON'T want?
- How can you make your outcome something you are aiming towards rather than something you are trying to move away from? (Instead of, *I wish my husband would stop ____ me*, say something like, *I want a relationship that is nurturing and respectful.*)
- WHY do you want this outcome?

Chapter 3

A Dangerous Mistake

A FEW YEARS AGO, I was in a dangerous, toxic "Christian" marriage and couldn't take it anymore! Very frightened of leaving my husband Brian, I believed if I stayed I might be dead by his initiative within a year. At least that was what people who knew him better than I warned me of. My close circle of confidants feared I would be the victim of a fatal "accident" by my husband. The police checked on me often to see if I was okay since I was too scared to file for a restraining order.

In time, I also had an additional worry. I received word that men, released from prison, were looking for Brian to settle a score since he had ratted on them, causing their incarceration. I worried about what would happen if they showed up at our isolated farm, especially since Brian was sporadic coming home. Would they hurt the children or me to send a message to Brian? I composed a letter to be found if they or Brian murdered me.

After months of agonizing over whether to stay or leave, a sickening discovery one morning prompted a final decision to flee. I loaded into my car some clothes, my mom's paintings, my three young daughters and their kittens, and a pet chicken named Lily. We drove across the country to my parents' home, hoping and praying for a better life.

If you are reading this book, it is possible that you are experiencing your own heart-breaking relationship. You most likely identify as a Christian. Your spouse may also consider himself Christian and justify his behavior with Bible verses.

While deciding whether to stay or leave a painful relationship is hard for anyone, ingrained, faulty religious beliefs compound a Christian victim's ability to get away from an abuser. It was a big issue I struggled with. I was more worried about disobeying God than I was of being murdered.

Do you identify with that feeling? Most Christian wives do. Our devotion to God and family is so strong that we will endure any hardship to keep heaven smiling upon us. The one thing that overrode my fear was the frightening realization of what would happen to my children if I weren't there to protect them. I decided that I loved my children too much to subject them to inevitable danger and abuse. If God's anger was to fall on me for no longer submitting to my husband's headship, well then, fall it must… I had to protect my daughters.

It was after I fled that God could help me see the truth about Him, and that He had never wanted the children or me to stay in that dangerous situation. I had stayed far longer than I needed to. Thankfully, I found the courage to leave when I did, and God guided us through the difficult days ahead.

Let me give you a little of my background. My parents raised me in a loving Christian home on a small farm in the dry eastern Oregon Outback. Our community economy was agriculture, timber and livestock. We had one flashing streetlight in town. My dad was a carpenter and my mom a homemaker. Since my siblings were at least

12 years older, I mostly grew up alone. I enjoyed playing with my stuffed animals and pets, climbing the haystack, playing in the barn and sneaking through the tall wheat that grew on our farm. I loved it when dad's Hereford cows calved because it sometimes meant a mama would need dad to turn her calf and pull it out. If I was lucky, a baby would need bottle fed for a while. Life couldn't get any better when mom and dad got me a beautiful Arabian mare who I named Pebbles. It was instant inseparable love and friendship between us.

I suppose that growing up with minimal media and friends (I was homeschooled) helped me develop a close relationship with God. I considered Him my best friend and spent hours talking to Him. After leaving home, I developed a habit of getting up early and fixing both of us a cup of hot chocolate. I would sit and read my Bible and talk to Him as I had always done. Sometimes if I decided to not get up and just sleep, I would feel Him tug at my heart as if to say, *Robin, get up! This is OUR time together!* The intense love I felt from Him, and the knowledge He enjoyed these quiet times together as much as I, always put a smile on my face and I gladly got up and poured us a cup of hot chocolate. These times of intimacy carried me through many dark days ahead, days I couldn't fathom would happen.

One day, a friend asked me to volunteer at the local women and children's crisis center. They needed extra help, and since I had time, would I please consider it? I said no. I had no experience with domestic violence and abuse and was sure I would not fit in or like it. I wanted to do other things with my life, but any door I tried to open seemed bolted shut. My friend continued to ask me for help and I went in just to get her to stop bugging me. I didn't realize it but God was directing my steps. This would become my life's work and passion.

Unfortunately, the wrong men attracted me. I learned all about the red flags of abusers and should have been able to avoid them, but couldn't. I continued life stuck in my own cycle of toxic relationships while helping others get free of theirs.

For me, the hardest part of working at the crisis center was that I didn't know how to help our toughest clients—Christian wives. These women returned to their abusive husbands because they believed God required them to do so. They thought they had to stay, submit and pray for their husbands. Often their husband was clergy or a community leader.

Sometimes our shelter referred inquiring Christian clients to a local pastor who had offered to counsel these women. What we didn't realize was that some pastors would counsel the women to go back home and submit per traditional religious teachings. I'm sure their intentions were good, but the result was bitter for these wives and their children.

I was, and am, a committed Christian myself. I wanted to please God, to be obedient to His Word, and to do the right thing for everyone involved. Like most others, I only knew the traditional church's teachings on wifely submission. I didn't know any other way. So the cycle for all of us continued.

At one point in between relationships, I ventured into the seemingly safe and fun world of Christian online dating. I met Brian there and his passionate relationship with God and traditional beliefs attracted me. Even though he had a shady past, his testimony of God's deliverance was miraculous and inspiring. Accustomed to hearing life-changing testimonies in church, it never occurred to me that Brian's testimony might not be authentic.

Brian seemed to know how to appeal to my spiritual side and challenged me to go deeper in my faith. I loved the intense Bible studies and prayer times we had, and I admired his grasp of the "deep" things of spiritual life. Ready to be a full-time mother and homemaker, I thought I had found a superb man and leader for our household. I thought I was leaving toxic relationships behind me forever.

Our story started out romantic and idealistic. It seemed so perfect we married within a couple months of meeting each other. But a few years later, as I shared previously, I was fleeing from him for my life. God didn't make me marry this guy, and in hindsight, I feel He tried to warn me against it. However, God stayed faithful to the children and I through the next few tumultuous years.

Since I didn't take the time to get to know Brian before marrying him, I got to know him afterwards. He had strange ideas such as wanting to move every three months to stay ahead of the police. I was unclear as to the reasoning in that since his incarceration was behind him. Brian also talked to a "guardian angel" called "Paul" and did whatever "Paul" told him to do regardless of my concerns. Brian would also feel undervalued at a job and quit on a whim. Whatever Brian did or said always had a spiritual motive and value to it. This included isolating me from family and friends because he believed they would try to break us up. He trusted no one and respected no one other than his grandfather, the person who had introduced him to drugs and violence at a young age.

When I would question something, Brian would show me how "religious" and in error I was, and how I needed to come to his side and be "spiritual." He took the time to show me from the Bible the fallacy of my thinking and ways. He believed since he was the head of the family, it was his responsibility to guide me in all things and I had to gratefully submit to it.

I figured it was better to just let Brian (and "Paul") do what they wanted since it didn't interfere with my being a happy full-time mom. I was content raising our two daughters, and as long as nothing took me away from them, I didn't worry too much about anything else. Brian was strange, but he provided for our needs. I thought life was good.

However, I was naïve. In hindsight, I should have been VERY worried. Following the birth of our third daughter, Brian gave up the Christian facade he had been using. I think he felt secure that I depended on him and was a mild-mannered, submissive, Christian wife. I wasn't going anywhere. The change in him progressed into a predictable cycle. Brian would hurt me or the kids in a new way and we made the adjustments to cope and hope that was the last. It never was.

Reflection: Regret

Regret. It can either disable you or propel you forward in life. Answer these questions to shift from powerlessness to desired change.

- In retrospect, what decisions and/or actions do you regret?
- Could you have acted any differently considering the particular stage in life you were in and the information you had?
- Would you change what happened and why?
- What real difference would that make in your life?
- What do your past decisions tell you about your personal values and perspective on life?
- What decisions are you now making that are influenced by regret?
- What did you do right in the situation that you regret?

Tips for Overcoming Regret

- Remember your humanity

    You did the best you knew how or were capable of at the time. Chances are you didn't have the resources, information or understanding you needed to do things differently back then. You felt you were making the best choice and that's all anyone can do. You are not perfect, but you are capable. Learning to bounce back comes with life experience, attitude and self-forgiveness.

- Learn from your mistakes

    When you realize you made a mistake, put your effort into fixing the situation if that is possible. Instead of beating yourself up with it, which helps nothing, look for the lessons. "Perfection" is not possible nor desirable. Learning is.

- Decide and act

    Good decision-making requires identifying the pros and cons of your options, knowing your values (Exercise A) and then moving forward with the BEST choice. Have faith you can make sound decisions and that you also can recover if it turns out to be less than ideal. If you regret an action, counteract it with an improved action. Remember, no matter how you've screwed up, you'll feel better if you are actively working to improve your situation.

- Focus forward

    Stop looking back. Quit thinking about what might have been if only you had done something differently. Imposing your current values and knowledge on your past self makes no sense. What's important is that your current values and knowledge align with what you are doing. Every time you catch yourself thinking one of those "if only I had…"

thoughts, STOP. Remind yourself that what's done is done and move on. Look for any positive aspects to the choices you made. Begin a practice of noticing what is good and the potential in front of you.

Foundation

"Therefore there is now no condemnation [no guilty verdict, no punishment] for those who are in Christ Jesus [who believe in Him as personal Lord and Savior]."

Romans 8:1 (AMP)

"Do not remember the former things, Or ponder the things of the past. Listen carefully, I am about to do a new thing, Now it will spring forth; Will you not be aware of it? I will even put a road in the wilderness, Rivers in the desert."

Isaiah 43:18-19 (AMP)

"…one thing I do: forgetting what lies behind and reaching forward to what lies ahead, I press on toward the goal to win the [heavenly] prize of the upward call of God in Christ Jesus. All of us who are mature [pursuing spiritual perfection] should have this attitude…"

Philippians 3:13-15 (AMP)

Chapter 4

The Crossroads of Redemption

WITHIN A YEAR of our third daughter's birth, Brian's thinking and behavior had reached a dangerous point. When our girls were just four, three and barely one, Brian took us to South America because "Paul" told him to. Brian assured me he had everything planned and it would be a great adventure. He had the funds to tide us over until he picked up work in construction or at a mission.

True, I had always seen him able to get work with little effort in a new place. Charm was his trademark and it got him pretty much anything he wanted. My gut told me though that this was not a good idea, and when I would cautiously share my concerns Brian would turn dark and angry. I was afraid to do anything other than go along with it.

Brian also told concerned people he planned to start an orphanage for kids. His motives appeared altruistic and his plans seemed at least possible. He would tell this to anybody who would listen and they would congratulate him on his bravery and sacrifice for the orphans in South America. They would tell me how lucky I was to have a selfless husband who cared so much about others.

I hoped they were right. I told myself that it would be fun and educational and we would come back to the States with great tales of our adventures. However, no matter how hard I tried to convince myself of this, my instincts worked overtime warning me otherwise. I was too afraid of Brian to do anything about it though, and didn't want to risk him taking the children without me.

The ability to stand up for what I believed was lost by now. We were two people in the flesh, but in every other way we were one person. We were Brian. He dominated and controlled the thinking, feeling and decision-making. I had lost my personal identity and soul to him and didn't even realize it.

After a month of wandering around Chile, we ended up penniless and homeless on a beach. Brian may have been able to get away with his charm and impulsive choices in the U.S., but the Chileans weren't buying it. Doors shut everywhere he turned. I felt exhausted, afraid, betrayed, hopeless, confused and angry. This appeared to be a tragic experience. Brian even gave up hope and told me to get used to being homeless, I would learn to like it!

Becoming homeless in a foreign country with three small children jarred me out of my spiritual and psychological lethargy. I had no choice but to see the reality of my life and the truth of what kind of man my husband was. My illusion of us being a normal, happy, good Christian family popped like a bubble that night on the sand.

I had reached a crossroads, knowing the choices I made in the next few hours and days would define the rest of our lives. I was not prepared for this in any way: mentally, financially, spiritually, emotionally... Why do crossroads happen when one is least ready for it?

When morning came, I went for a walk on the beach as the sun warmed the chilly damp air. Stepping around sleeping bodies, I pondered how my life was turning out and how my daughters were being affected. It was not what I wanted for us. But there was no denying, as I took a ruthless look at my life, that the only reason for it was because I had made my own unwise choices. No one had ever held a gun to my head and made me do anything. Sure, I had my share of unfair life circumstances. Until that morning, it had made sense to blame other things and people for my unhappiness. But that morning on the beach I admitted that I was responsible for being there.

The great thing about accepting responsibility, I discovered, was that it gave me the power to change my life if I didn't like it! I took ownership of my life and choices. What was done was done up to that point. I couldn't change the past, but it didn't mean I had to accept it as my future. It was the most freeing and empowering awakening I had ever experienced. As I took ownership of my life and choices, I realized that I would have to stand up to Brian and stop doing whatever he demanded.

I knew the girls and I needed divine help and expected Brian to fight me on my new independence. I was supposed to be submissive and follow him even if he demanded we live homeless. However, despite that ingrained and faulty religious mindset, I sensed that God would somehow help me. I knew I was doing the right thing to protect my girls.

Before going back to our little shelter, I prayed one of the most heartfelt prayers I have ever prayed: "Help us God!" My inner pain and fear were so overwhelming that I couldn't choke out much more. But I knew God heard and understood the unspoken words in it.

I also resolved to put God back on the throne of my heart. Brian had usurped that place that should only belong to God. Without understanding the dynamics and meaning of everything yet, I knew two things for sure that morning: 1, God needed to be first place in my heart; and 2, I needed to protect my children.

Gathering all the courage I could muster, I walked back to Brian and the girls. I told him with a firm resolution that surprised me: "We will NOT spend another night out here. I'm getting us back home." Brian shocked me by resignedly nodding his head, allowing me to take the lead. That scared me worse than if he had argued with me! It terrified me to take on this new role of an assertive woman, and I was angry that I had to learn how to do it here of all places and times. I had no idea how to get us out of the mess we were in when we had not a cent left and had alienated our friends and family. Even the local churches and missions had rejected us. The task before me seemed impossible.

God honored my choice to put Him back into first place in my life and to protect my daughters. He directed my steps that day, brought provision, and in two weeks we were all back home in the States without having spent another night outside.

I thought life couldn't get any worse than what I had experienced on that trip but was wrong. I wanted to go home, forget that nightmare, and resume the decent life I had known before. However, after we arrived back in the States, the following year became a worse nightmare as Brian spiraled into a cruel and dangerous dark hole that threatened again to destroy us all.

There is a common belief that adversity makes a person stronger. Brian proved this is a myth. The *right response* to adversity makes a person stronger. And wiser. Brian's response to the disaster in South America was to discard any semblance of goodness. He chose anger, bitterness and blaming, and engaged in dangerous behavior that hurt anyone unfortunate to be in his path.

As I mentioned at the beginning, I made a strategic plan of escape, and with the support of a few others, followed through. I did not have my life mapped out and the following year as a single mom without financial support from my furious husband was difficult. Sometimes life was so hard and discouraging I thought I had made a mistake and it would be better to go back just to have provision and stability. But through the grace of God, we made it without that happening.

Today, I am free of toxic relationships and my children are thriving. I believe our happiness and hope is all because of a loving God who must have cheered to see me leave the abuse. I had plenty of obstacles to face though:

- The country was in a recession and government resources were dwindling.
- My husband was dangerously angry and refused to contribute financially to us.
- Years of being without a job hindered my being able to reenter the workforce.
- I was confused about love. I scorned the one man who offered me true love and respect, while being drawn back into the cycle of toxic relationships with "exciting" men who wanted to "protect" me.
- I needed to rebuild strained relationships that my husband had nearly destroyed.
- I had to help my children and myself heal and recover in the midst of the crushing stress of trying to start life anew.

God's grace, forgiveness and love not only allowed us to change course, but to do it with His blessing and help. We experienced the truth of Romans 8:28, *"We know that all things work together for good for those who love God, who are called according to His purpose."*

In hindsight, that painful crossroad opened the door to the

greatest opportunities. It was a disguised invitation to a life of peace and happiness.

You may be at your own crossroads. Life may seem hopeless, confusing and unfair. Fear and uncertainty may color every moment. GOD LOVES YOU. He wants you to feel safe, loved, treasured and honored.

Remember what I said about having hot chocolate with Him? He wants this close fellowship with you as well. You may do something other than talk over cocoa, but whatever it is, take the time to be with Him. As you draw near to Him, having faith He loves, accepts and approves of you, you will get the strength and help you need.

James 4:8 promises, *"Draw near to God, and He will draw near to you…"* and Isaiah 41:10, *"Do not fear, for I am with you, do not be afraid, for I am your God; I will strengthen you, I will help you, I will uphold you with My victorious right hand."*

God cherishes you, His daughter. Take Zephaniah 3:17 to heart. Hear your heavenly Father whispering to you, *Daughter, I am in your midst, a Warrior who saves. I rejoice over you with joy; you will be quiet in My love.*

Reflection: Responsibility

Responsibility. I talked about the first lesson I learned that got me through my crisis in Chile: taking ownership of my life. This is the starting point when you are in a crisis and does not condemn or weaken you. It empowers you!

"To the person you give responsibility, you give power." That includes power over you. You have the power to change your life if you don't like it. Taking responsibility is the starting point for growth and change in your life. This becomes fun once you realize you will make progress in a desirable direction.

Marriage does not absolve you of the consequences of your choices. Even not choosing and being passive is still a choice, one you now live with. With the "burden of responsibility" comes the freedom of living your life fully.

- What would you do if you didn't have to live with the consequences?
- Which choice or decision are you avoiding?
- If you still don't think you have a choice, PRETEND you do. What would you do?
- Suppose fear does not exist in your world. What could you do now?
- What would you do if you knew you couldn't fail?
- What could you do if you didn't care what other people thought?

Tips for Taking Responsibility

We are all responsible for our own actions or inactivity. Your husband cannot blame his parents or you when he gives an account to God someday. You won't be able to blame your husband. That's good news! I can't imagine being responsible for other's bad choices. I'm thankful that I can be forgiven for where I have blown it and Jesus offers another chance and His help to do what often seems impossible under the circumstances.

As a Christian, our first loyalty is to Christ. NOT our husband. I will prove this biblically in the next few chapters. The Bible is overflowing with the intervention of God into the lives of all who put Him first. Your husband is just a man, and on the wrong side of

God. That's not your responsibility to fix. He is making his choices. Take refuge in Christ and He will help you do what is best for you and give you the wisdom to know how.

- Identify where you need to take responsibility. What is holding you back the most in your life right now?
- Say often to yourself, *I am responsible for my choices!* Embrace the tension and energy that comes with this new power. You are in charge now and you can change your situation.
- Recognize you DO have a choice. Reject the lie of *"I don't/didn't have a choice…"* It may be unpleasant but you do have a choice in the matter. Make a list of things you can do now to move toward what you want.
- Commit to changing your life and act on one thing. What one thing can you do today or tomorrow?

***You may not know what your options are in a relationship crisis. An important first action you can take is to talk to someone who can help you identify options. Talk to an advocate at your local shelter or call a hot-line or reach out to me. I include helpful resources for this at the end of the book.

Foundation

"For all must carry their own loads."

Galatians 6:5 (NRSV)

"So then, each of us will give an account of himself to God."

Romans 14:12 (AMP)

"Whatever you do [whatever your task may be], work from the soul [that is, put in your very best effort], as [something done] for the Lord and not for men, knowing [with all certainty] that it is from the Lord [not from men] that you will receive the inheritance which is your [greatest] reward. It is the Lord Christ whom you [actually] serve."

Colossians 3:23-24 (AMP)

"And Jesus replied to him, "'You shall love the Lord your God with all your heart, and with all your soul, and with all your mind.'"

Matthew 22:37 (AMP)

Chapter 5

Abusive or Ignorant?

"Nothing in all the world is more dangerous than sincere ignorance and conscientious stupidity."

~ Martin Luther King, Jr.

WAS MY HUSBAND just a jerk or was there a more serious character flaw? I asked myself this often. It was hard to decipher, since our relationship started out exciting and fun, and we enjoyed many good times together. As the years went by, Brian's behavior was increasingly hurtful. My emotional health seemed to hang on by the thinnest of threads. I wondered, am I losing my mind or am I in a dysfunctional and perhaps dangerous relationship?

Dr. Jeanne King, author of *All But My Soul: Abuse Beyond Control*, explains the difference well:

> I think being abusive is a rather general way of describing behavior that violates you as a person; your rights, your space, your choices, yourself. It can come out of frustration,

stress, lowered inhibitions, insecurity, fear, vulnerability, or any combination of the above.

Being an abuser, on the other hand, in the classical sense, refers to a person that fulfills a specific criteria. And when engaged in an intimate relationship with this person, a specific criteria of defining characteristics exist which are "intimate partner violence."

The criteria for intimate partner violence consists of: possessiveness, controlling behavior, lack of empathy, externalization of blame, isolation of victimized partner, and the use of battering to create and maintain a relationship of unequal power. (2)

That is the primary difference between those who are challenging because they don't know better, and those who are abusive out of a need to control. There can be many things that cause people to behave in hurtful ways such as drug use, stress, financial pressure and illness.

Many people have not learned how to treat others with integrity and decency because it hasn't been modeled for them. They unintentionally cause others pain because that's what they know. However, they are not trying to gain power and control over others. They don't understand how to speak and act in a way that is beneficial and respectful. Counseling, education and mentoring can change this for a happier future.

Abuse, however, is a mentality of entitlement. Abusers rarely respond well to counseling and education because they do not see themselves as part of a problem. Their goal is power and control over others regardless of what it takes to get it and keep it. Unhampered by a healthy conscience, they steal a victim's identity. Some, like me, see it as a form of murder.

As I shared earlier, I had lost my identity to Brian. It happened so subtly that I didn't even recognize the process. Brian did all of our thinking and decision-making. When our relationship first started, I saw this as being strong, protective and decisive. It was masculine, romantic and flattering. As time went by, I occasionally asserted my independent opinion about something only to be punished. I learned it was better to just accept what he demanded for the sake of peace.

It was at my crossroads in Chile that I realized how much control he had taken of me. I realized I no longer knew myself as a distinct individual. I had a feeling that somewhere along the line I had died, without knowing when or how it had happened. Realizing this was a significant part of my awakening into the person I am today.

Think abuse is limited to physical violence? It's not. Brian never laid a hand on me violently, but he controlled and terrorized me. He used tactics of emotional, financial, social, sexual and spiritual abuse to keep me in line with what he wanted.

The THREAT of physical violence was there. I remember him preparing and serving me dinner one day. While we ate, he "joked" about knowing how to kill with a local herb placed in food and it appearing like a natural heart attack to a coroner. He "joked" about slicing pets throats when he tired of them. He tried to poison our neighbor's pets. He seemed to be able to get away with whatever he did.

If he felt a neighbor or business associate had crossed him, he planned their "accidental" death. He would even demand I pass along his threats of murder to men he believed had flirted with me. So no, he never had to punch me in the face. It scared me knowing what he was capable of. I did nothing that might arouse violent anger toward the kids or myself.

Lundy Bancroft, author of *Why Does He Do That? Inside the*

Minds of Angry and Controlling Men, offers this if you are still wondering about the violence issue:

> Has he ever trapped you in a room and not let you out?
>
> Has he ever raised a fist as if he were going to hit you?
>
> Has he ever thrown an object that hit you or nearly did?
>
> Has he ever held you down or grabbed you to restrain you?
>
> Has he ever shoved, poked, or grabbed you?
>
> Has he ever threatened to hurt you?
>
> If the answer to any of these questions is yes, then we can stop wondering whether he'll ever be violent; he already has been. (3)

Understanding what makes up abuse and toxicity is important to making good choices about your relationship. We don't want to label people as abusers without there being a pattern of abusive behavior.

However, if the signs of abuse are there, then it is better to accept that and move forward. Ignoring or justifying it will only cause more turmoil and pain. Often, it ends in tragedy. As hard as it may be to consider that your husband is an abuser, it will still help you and maybe him to acknowledge it.

As said in John 8:32, *"and you will know the truth, and the truth will make you free."* Be open to the truth about your spouse and your relationship. Then you will be on your way to getting the answers and help you need.

If you have not, it would be worth your time to read the interview of Lundy Bancroft at *Pandora's Project*. Louise, the interviewer, asked him about how to recognize the signs of abuse:

> **Louise:** Some of our members are really hard on themselves

because they didn't recognize the signs of an abuser. Yet you've written that there is no one stereotype of an abuser - could you elaborate on that?

Lundy: Abusers don't usually show themselves early in a relationship—they can look pretty much like other men as dating is beginning. There are things you can watch for, but they aren't usually things anyone warned you about, so it's not your fault that you didn't know they were danger signs. Here are a few of them:

- Jealousy and possessiveness, which can be flattering, but are actually really bad news.
- Being controlling.
- Always making everything your fault.
- He seems to be on really bad terms with his former partners.
- He seems to have bad attitudes toward women in general.
- He gets really disrespectful at times, then makes excuses for it.
- He does things you asked him not to do, perhaps too many favors for example, and it's hard to back him off.
- He pressures you regarding sex, such as wanting sex sooner in the relationship than you do.
- He's self-focused and doesn't show that much interest in your tastes or opinions.
- He gets intimidating when he's angry and then blames that on you.

There are various others, but these are critical ones to begin with. (4)

I want to emphasize that abusers don't show up holding a sign announcing their intentions. Even though I was a domestic violence advocate, I still missed or justified the signs with Brian. So please don't beat yourself up over it. Be forgiving and kind to yourself and focus on what you can do now to change your future.

Some behavior I considered "mostly good" that was abusive and controlling. As a positive person who easily forgives, I had no problem focusing on the good things about Brian. After a while I focused on them more out of a need to survive than believing in his goodness. Abusers are adept at acting good and caring when it serves their purpose. Family and neighbors often remember criminals with fondness. Even with my professional training I ignored far too many signs. I can see that now but could not, or would not, face it back then.

For example, one lie of Brian's I believed was his explanation for his mysterious disappearances. Brian would disappear during the night without a word he was leaving, where he was going, or how long he would be gone. I didn't know what to tell questioning people or our children. It was bewildering and heart-breaking to experience as things spiraled more out of control.

I hated his disappearances and worried, wondering what was happening and why he would do this to us. When he would come home, he would say something to this effect: *Honey, I needed to get away to study my Bible and pray. You know when there is a special calling on someone's life, like there is on mine, that we have to obey God and hide ourselves away with Him when He calls. You have to accept that when God calls me away to be alone with Him, I have to go. I shouldn't have to explain that to you.*

The concept of courtesy escaped him. I'm embarrassed now to say I thought, though rude, he really was going off to pray. In hindsight, I realize that I was naïve of the signs of drug use/binges. I also ignored my gut instincts telling me what my mind couldn't comprehend. My naivete didn't make his behavior good. It was a lie and hurtful to the children and myself.

Another thing he would tell me sometimes was that he was discipling a new employee at work. This required staying at work late, sometimes even overnight. Brian would share stories of the employee's progress and growth as a Christian under his wise guidance. As I write this, I shake my head with disgust I believed these stories. Although, who wouldn't be supportive of helping someone who is troubled and needs encouragement? I supported it. I wanted to believe it. What a good man Brian was to sacrificially help others! I would come to realize much later that the only "discipling" Brian was doing was drugging and partying with his new buddy.

Jealousy was another trap for me. In the beginning, Brian made his jealousy appear masculine, noble and loving. But it never was good and never was love. Jealousy is abuse and fatal for many.

My intuition knew something was amiss, but until my mind could understand, I didn't know what else to do but accept the explanation offered. In hindsight, I wish I had trusted my intuition and talked to someone who might have had insight into why I was feeling so bad about things so noble.

Consider that what you think might be justifiable behavior might be abusive or at least toxic. It might be a warning flag of upcoming trouble. Talking to a third party, like an advocate at a women's shelter, can present other possibilities to consider.

Many people around us could see what Brian was doing and what a jerk he was. But Brian's conditioning and isolating had me believing I could trust no one. I believed him that we had a love so special and beautiful that inferior people would try to destroy it out of jealousy. The problem was, in Brian's world, everyone was inferior. I avoided people and was defensive at any suggestion Brian was less than perfect. People kept their concerns to themselves even though they saw plenty to worry about.

Reflection: Acceptance

Acceptance. Is it time to accept the reality of your situation? Acceptance embraces what is happening now and admits that you cannot control or change others. But it doesn't stop there! You don't have to like what is happening and you are not resigning yourself to injustice, violence or abuse. It means you are ready to acknowledge the truth and take appropriate action. Acceptance empowers you to move toward the change you desire.

- Ask others who have a more objective view: What do you think about this? What am I missing?
- What am I doing that's helping?
- What am I doing that's getting in my way?
- How would I react if this were happening to my friend?
- What advice would I give her?
- In what way are the consequences of this problem felt?
- What might happen if I do nothing and just ignore this problem?
- When might this problem become even bigger?
- What might lead to a negative outcome?
- How would this potentially affect you, others and your life?
- Could resolving this problem cause other problems for you? Why? Why not?

Tips for Radical Acceptance

- Accept your current situation

    It will make you happier now, lift off a load of stress and self-condemnation, and lead to a better future. Living a lie is harder than facing reality. Working with reality will help you make decisions that will change your life.

- Be honest

    When you can admit that your desired version of life is not reality, you can create a new future. Instead of focusing on what you think your life should be, work on creating the life you want. Dealing with the bad parts will open the door to the goodness of life you crave. Bring your desires to Christ in prayer.

- Accept the struggle

    Struggle is inevitable if you want something different from what you have. Embrace it! On the other side of the fear, discomfort and struggle is what you want. Yet in the struggle, hold on tightly to God's peace and lean into His strength to get through the struggle.

- Make a plan and include a support system

    Your new reality can start to take shape once you have a plan with specific goals and supportive people to help you achieve them. Choose wisely who you confide in. Reach out to those who understand the special dynamics you are living with and will support you. It's usually good to talk to your local women's shelter first.

Foundation

"Do not be anxious or worried about anything, but in everything [every circumstance and situation] by prayer and petition with thanksgiving, continue to make your [specific] requests known to God. And the peace of God [that peace which reassures the heart, that peace] which transcends

all understanding, [that peace which] stands guard over your hearts and your minds in Christ Jesus [is yours]."

Philippians 4:6-7 (AMP)

"You will keep in perfect and constant peace the one whose mind is steadfast [that is, committed and focused on You—in both inclination and character], Because he trusts and takes refuge in You [with hope and confident expectation]."

Isaiah 26:3 (AMP)

"Without consultation and wise advice, plans are frustrated, But with many counselors they are established and succeed."

Proverbs 15:22 (AMP)

Chapter 6

Isolation Is Dangerous

ISOLATION IS A hallmark of abuse. Abusers make separation seem good, reasonable and even spiritual. If you are avoiding people, or are being kept from socializing with others, wake up! You are in an unhealthy relationship and it will not get better.

A husband who loves you and has nothing to hide will not "protect" you from family, friends and community. He may express concern over an issue with someone, but his intention will not be to tell you what you have to do. Rather, healthy couples talk about people and issues in a respectful and supportive manner.

There is no justification for isolation. Isolation is what delusional and insecure people do to get and maintain power over others. This happens in cults and other unhealthy groups.

Jesus doesn't promote this. The Bible encourages meeting with others for many reasons. Socializing is an important part of our growth. If your husband is telling you otherwise, he is telling you something that goes against the Bible.

Consider these biblical principles of sharing life with others:

- Loving others as we love ourselves by showing deliberate and purposeful respect, goodwill and benevolent concern. (Mark 12:26-31; John 13:34-35, 15:12; Romans 15:1-2)

- Self-righteousness and arrogance are displayed when we treat others as inferior. God hates self-righteousness! (Romans 3:21-24; 1 John 1:8; Luke 18:9-14; Isaiah 5:21; Galatians 6:1-3)

- Generosity toward others with our time and money. Generosity is not just about writing out a check and walking away. God's generosity includes taking the time to talk with others, coming alongside them and helping them in their struggles. (1 John 3:17; 1 Timothy 6:17-19; Isaiah 58:10-11)

We need each other to be healthy. Being alone goes against God's principles of maturity in believers. Jesus modeled it for us. He wasn't an island to Himself. He socialized with men, women and children inside and outside the religious institution, showing great care and interest in them and their lives.

Brian believed everyone was against us because we had something so special they were jealous. If they weren't jealous, then they were "ignorant" or "religious." Or people were against us because we were the "chosen" of God and they weren't, and we had to live untainted lives apart from them. Does your husband display any of these arrogant attitudes?

The fact is, it is unlikely that everyone in your world wants to ruin your life and marriage. People aren't just sitting around wallowing in jealousy over your relationship, or trying to destroy your happiness to make themselves feel better. Most people are good, kind and want you to be happy and safe. Most people want to get along and believe the best. However, people also have the objective freedom to see red flags in someone else's relationship. If people seem concerned about things, there is probably a good reason for it!

On the flip side, many church members and leaders turn a blind eye to abuse, even blaming the victim for it. This is common so please do not make them the defining standard for what is or isn't appropriate behavior. You are more likely to get valuable feedback from people not attending your church, such as coworkers, support groups, helping agencies, friends and acquaintances.

Another red flag I ignored was isolation from his family. When we met, Brian claimed his family was corrupt and therefore it was necessary to protect me from them. He painted a picture of gross dysfunction, lying and unfairness that made me feel sorry for him and never want to be around them. I couldn't believe how evil they were and why they would ever want to hurt him and our relationship. Brian was fortunate to have gotten away from such terrible people!

I should have recognized that as the red flag of an abuser it was. But Brian always had compelling reasons for everything. It wasn't until the end of our marriage I realized they had been lies designed to keep me protected from the truth his family and friends would have warned me of.

I found out after I left him he had also told them terrible lies about me to keep them from wanting to talk to me. His family was distant and distrustful of me even though I had never been involved in any of the things Brian claimed about me. By lying to all of us, he protected himself from exposure.

See how smooth and clever abusers are? They must keep the truth suppressed! That is done by controlling information and manipulating people and events so it does not expose them. Until the end I couldn't grasp that Brian's testimony could be false. It was the hardest thing for me to comprehend, a fake testimony! I'll talk about this more soon.

It was after I found out the lies he had told about me to his family I realized Brian had fooled all of us. It worked for quite a while, but God caused the truth to surface. Brian was polished, smart and a complete fraud. But all I saw was what he wanted me to see: a strong and gifted man of God protecting his family.

Reflection: Isolation

Isolation. It's one of the deepest, most painful expressions of unworthiness. Being monitored, isolated and stalked changes you. If you are introverted, then it's even harder to reach out, but it's important to include good people in your life. It can take a long time to recover from an abusive relationship, but including other people who love and support your recovery speeds it up.

- What's standing in your way of connecting with other people?
- What do you need/want to do to get there?
- What do you have to offer others? What is one way you can move toward doing that?

Tips for Connecting with Others

- Work on connecting with others, even in small ways

  Victims of abuse suffer from a lack of self-worth that keeps them alone. Thoughts like "I don't have anything to offer" keep them from volunteering at their local food bank or caring for animals at a shelter. A rewarding first step to enlarging your world is to volunteer. Think about issues you care about and look up organizations that do that. Consider volunteering at your local women's shelter too! Make that first call to them or drop by. It may be hard but you can do it and the reward will be huge!

- What assumptions are you making that includes the thought or feeling you must do it alone?

  One of the best ways to bring clarity to these false assumptions is to talk it out with someone. We all need someone we can talk to who will reflect to us the truth or error of what we are thinking. If you do not have someone like that yet, join a local domestic violence support group. You will meet wonderful people who you can talk to and develop quality friendships with.

- Express yourself

  Dance. Paint. Garden. Craft. It's time to rediscover what you love and who you are. Your abuser took these from you. Take them back and do them again. As you open to your creative side, share it with others.

- Talk about it

  Sharing your story can heal and empower. I know it did for me. Just sharing my story in a blog led me to here with you. Perhaps start with a diary then talk to someone who you know will be supportive. Telling your story helps you cope with your changing feelings and also helps others. Your abuser took away your voice. Take it back!

- Reclaim other activities you love

  Do you love to work out? Go to the gym or join a group that is doing what you enjoy. MeetUp.com is a good place to find local people who are doing what they love together. Want to meet other mom's and do things with your kids? There are groups for everyone. Seek and you will find!

Foundation

"I can do all things [which He has called me to do] through Him who strengthens and empowers me [to fulfill His purpose—I am self-sufficient in Christ's sufficiency; I am ready for anything and equal to anything through Him who infuses me with inner strength and confident peace.]"

Philippians 4:13 (AMP)

"For the Lord will be your confidence, firm and strong, And will keep your foot from being caught [in a trap]."

Proverbs 3:26 (AMP)

"But He has said to me, "My grace is sufficient for you [My loving-kindness and My mercy are more than enough—always available—regardless of the situation]; for[My] power is being perfected [and is completed and shows itself most effectively] in [your] weakness." Therefore, I will all the more gladly boast in my weaknesses, so that the power of Christ [may completely enfold me and] may dwell in me."

2 Corinthians 12:9 (AMP)

Chapter 7

Where Is Your Marriage on This Scale?

"Let the wife make the husband glad to come home, and let him make her sorry to see him leave."

~ Martin Luther

LET'S LOOK AT where your marriage may be on a scale of HEALTHY to STRUGGLING to TOXIC.

HEALTHY

There is no such thing as a 'perfect marriage.' However, a couple in a healthy marriage enjoys a good partnership. Some characteristics of a healthy marriage are:

- You both feel happy and safe, alone and together
- You still go on adventures together

- Open and honest communication dominate
- You can laugh and de-escalate conflicts when they arise
- You solve differences of opinion through listening and compromise
- You have mutual and separate friends
- There are goals for the future and you work together to achieve them
- You celebrate each other's success
- You both take responsibility for the good and the bad and strategize how to overcome the bad
- You give each other space
- You both forgive and can say, "I'm sorry."
- Neither habitually engages in negative attitudes of criticism, contempt, defensiveness or stonewalling
- There is acceptance of each other with no demand to change
- You motivate each other to pursue dreams and live life to the fullest
- You help each other with parenting and chores

STRUGGLING

As we move into the middle, there are marriages that struggle. Most marriages do at times and there is always room for growth. *These relationships are characterized more by what is absent rather than what is abusive.*

Ignorance and immaturity cause a struggle. Circumstances outside of control contribute to stress. Knowledge, time and maturity usually makes things right. A couple can work through these problems by studying God's Word and getting competent counseling or other professional services as appropriate. Sometimes there is an underlying health issue that needs addressed, or financial and communication issues that can be resolved with professional guidance. There is a solution for the source of the struggle, and both marriage partners want to find out what it is and resolve the problem, or at least learn how to deal with it in a positive way.

If you fall into this middle category, please do not use this book to rationalize giving up on your marriage. Prayerfully examine your motives. Although you may be unhappy in your current relationship, it is better to stay and work through the problems. It can be turned around if you are both willing!

TOXIC

Marriages that fall into this extreme are the focus of this book. Your spouse, through the intentional use of pain and intimidation, has breached the marriage covenant dangerously and destructively. It is for Christian women who find themselves trapped in fear and false theology I strive to shine the light of God's truth to dispel the darkness.

Characteristics of a toxic marriage are:

- You feel afraid of and eager to please your husband to avoid problems
- You go along with whatever he says and does to keep the peace
- You check in often with him to report where you are and what you are doing
- He monitors you
- He has a temper and is possessive
- He has been physically violent toward you, children or pets

- He sabotages your job, school or social occasions
- He restricts you from seeing family and friends
- You rarely go out in public without your husband or being monitored
- You have limited access to money, credit cards or the car
- You are experiencing personality changes, such as going from outgoing to withdrawn
- You feel depressed, anxious, drained, scared, ashamed, confused or suicidal
- He uses dominance, humiliation, isolation, threats, intimidation, denial and blame to manipulate you
- You wonder if you are crazy and the one to blame for all the problems
- He forces or coerces you into things you don't want, including sexually

Appendix A tells some signs of chronic personality problems and Appendix C gives a risk assessment to see if your relationship falls into this dangerous category.

Despite the drama and excitement surrounding Brian's supposed conversion and transformation, he could not hold to basic Christian tenants over the long haul. Matthew 7:15-21 says we can know the character of someone by their actions. In the next chapter, let's see if we can get more clarity by examining your husband's "fruit" in the light of God's Word.

Reflection: Boundaries

Boundaries. They define and protect us as individuals in a relationship. Below are questions to help you evaluate your marriage.

Remember, in a healthy relationship, each partner enhances the couple's life and receives the benefits of their joint efforts. Both value the other's contributions and express respect, appreciation, support and love to each other.

- Your daughter is you in your relationship. She asks you if she should stay or leave. What do you tell her?
- Your husband says he has to work late. Do you believe him?
- You have to explain to your children years from now why staying with their dad was good for them and you. Will they agree?
- Though there have been problems, can you honestly tell your kids their dad is worthy of respect?
- Your daughter or granddaughter wants to marry a man just like your husband. Do you feel happy for her?
- Does your husband make you and the kids feel safe, or do you walk on eggshells?
- Does your husband support your personal interests and goals?
- Despite differences, does your husband apologize if he sees he has hurt your feelings?

Tips for Developing Boundaries

- Know what your limits are

    Think about what is making you feel uncomfortable or stressed. Now rate your feeling from 1 to 10; with ten meaning you are very stressed over it. If you rate your feeling as 6 or above, this indicates you need to set a boundary. What is it about the situation that is bothering you? Do you feel someone else is imposing their expectations, views or values on you and you resent it?

- Figure out your values

    If you are struggling with the boundary issue, shift to thinking about your values. Pick your top 3 core values and create boundaries that support them. For example, one of your core values might be kindness. A person rude to the waitress is not compatible with your value of kindness. This would cause you to limit your time with them and set the boundary that when with you, you will not tolerate unkindness to others including toward yourself. If your husband is the one who is unkind, this tells you that you are sacrificing your value to accommodate him, leading to your stress and unhappiness. Either confront this, accommodate it, or end it. You will only be happy as long as your values are being honored. Exercise A is a values exercise to help with this.

- Give yourself permission to set limits

    It's common to feel fear, guilt and self-doubt when we think of setting limits. Fear of the other person's response, or guilt for saying no, can disable feelings. Maybe you don't feel you deserve to take care of yourself. Boundaries are not just for you though. They signal self-respect for yourself and for others. Everyone wins when you know your limits and enforce them. They also tell you who doesn't deserve to be in your life. Healthy people recognize and respect other's boundaries besides their own.

- Start small and have the support of others

    Boundary setting is a learned skill. It's okay to start small and grow. You don't have to have it all figured out right now. Pick one core value. With the support of someone else, decide on one assertive thing you can do to support that value in your life and relationship. Be proactive about taking a small step as often as possible, recognizing what matters to you and setting a limit on what you tolerate.

- Avoid this common unhealthy boundary

  If your boundary includes the words "always" or "never" it may be unrealistic and won't last. "I expect a call if you will be late for dinner or I may eat without you," is a reasonable boundary. "I will never fix you dinner again if you don't call me if you will be late," is manipulative and unrealistic.

- Detach

  You can be open and attached to others yet keep personal space that minimizes emotional and psychological entanglement. Everyone has different boundaries and values (some have none). You are a separate individual from everyone else, including your spouse. Being married does not make enmeshment a required or good thing. Value yourself enough to take care of yourself.

Foundation

Jesus modeled healthy boundaries. There is an excellent article on this at www.soulshepherding.org/jesus-set-boundaries/. Here are a few examples from author Bill Gaultiere's article:

Jesus Said No to Inappropriate Behavior:

- Demands. He withdrew from the crowds who wanted Him, for one-on-one time with the Father. (Luke 5:15-16)
- Abuse. He fought His way through the crowd that was trying to throw Him off a cliff for claiming to be the Messiah. (Luke 4:28-30)
- Entitlement. He didn't give in to His mother and brothers

who tried to use their relationship with Him to pull Him away from the crowd He was ministering to. (Matthew 12:46-50)

- Baiting Questions. When the religious leaders asked Him baiting questions to make Him look foolish He answered with incisive questions of His own. (Matthew 21:23-27, 22:15-22)

- Cynicism. He said no to Herod's mocking demand, "Show us a sign that you are the Son of God." (Luke 23:8-9)

- Manipulation. He said no to Peter and the disciples who had an inappropriate agenda for Jesus to be a political king or military warrior rather than a sacrificial lamb. (Matthew 16:23)

- Pride. He didn't heal those who were too proud to trust Him. (Matthew 13:58)

Chapter 8

Is His Fruit Good or Toxic?

"Beware of false prophets, who come to you in sheep's clothing but inwardly are ravenous wolves. You will know them by their fruits. Are grapes gathered from thorns, or figs from thistles? In the same way, every good tree bears good fruit, but the bad tree bears bad fruit. A good tree cannot bear bad fruit, nor can a bad tree bear good fruit. Every tree that does not bear good fruit is cut down and thrown into the fire. Thus you will know them by their fruits. Not everyone who says to Me, 'Lord, Lord,' will enter the kingdom of heaven, but only the one who does the will of My Father in heaven."

~ Jesus (Matthew 7:15-21)

According to Barnes notes on this passage:

> Verse 15:... A false prophet is a teacher of incorrect doctrine, or one falsely and unjustly laying claims to divine inspiration... Who come in sheep's clothing... The sheep is an emblem of innocence, sincerity and harmlessness. To come in sheep's clothing is to assume the appearance of sanctity and

innocence, when the heart is evil. Ravening wolves... they assumed the appearance of holiness in order that they might the more readily get the property of the people...

Verse 16: Ye shall know them by their fruits - The Savior gives the proper test of their character. People do not judge of a tree by its leaves, or bark or flowers, but by the fruit which it bears. The flowers may be beautiful and fragrant, the foliage thick and green; but these are merely ornamental. It is the "fruit" that is of chief service to man; and he forms his opinion of the nature and value of the tree by that fruit. So of pretensions to religion. The profession may be fair; but the "conduct" - the fruit - is to determine the nature of the principles.

Verse 17: A corrupt tree - The word "corrupt" here does not signify, as our translation would seem to indicate, that the tree "had been" good, but had become "vitiated;" but that it was a tree of a useless character, of a nature that produced nothing beneficial.

Verse 21: The Savior goes on to say that many, on the ground of a mere profession such as He had just referred to, would claim admittance into His kingdom. See Matthew 7:21; 1 Corinthians 1:26; 1 Corinthians 13:1-3... In this last place, Paul says that, though he spoke with the tongue of angels, and had the gift of prophecy, and could remove mountains, but had not charity or love, all would be of no avail. (5)

Wow! Talk about an accurate description of many religious and abusive husbands. Brian was "a teacher of incorrect doctrine," "falsely and unjustly laying claims to divine inspiration," with "the appearance of sanctity and innocence, when the heart is evil," and "... assumed the appearance of holiness in order that they might the more readily get the property of the people." Here, I would substitute "soul" for "property." Isn't that what abusers do? They steal our identity, our very soul from us.

In 2 Corinthians 13:5 Paul commanded, *"Examine yourselves to see whether you are living in the faith. Test yourselves. Do you not realize that Jesus Christ is in you? Unless, indeed, you fail to meet the test!"*

Jesus shows us what it means to "meet the test" of living in the faith in John 15:1-17,

"I am the true vine, and My Father is the vine grower. He removes every branch in Me that bears no fruit. Every branch that bears fruit He prunes to make it bear more fruit. You have already been cleansed by the word that I have spoken to you. Abide in Me as I abide in you. Just as the branch cannot bear fruit by itself unless it abides in the vine, neither can you unless you abide in Me.

I am the vine, you are the branches. Those who abide in Me and I in them bear much fruit because apart from Me you can do nothing. Whoever does not abide in Me is thrown away like a branch and withers; such branches are gathered, thrown into the fire, and burned.

If you abide in Me, and My words abide in you, ask for whatever you wish, and it will be done for you. My Father is glorified by this, that you bear much fruit and become My disciples. As the Father has loved Me, so I have loved you; abide in My love. If you keep My commandments, you will abide in My love, just as I have kept My Father's commandments and abide in His love.

I have said these things to you so that My joy may be in you, and that your joy may be complete. This is My commandment, that you love one another as I have loved you. No one has greater love than this, to lay down one's life for one's friends. You are My friends if you do what I command you. I do not call you servants any longer, because the servant does not know what the master is doing; but I have called you friends because I have made known to you everything that I have heard from My Father.

You did not choose Me but I chose you. And I appointed you to go and bear fruit, fruit that will last, so that the Father will give you whatever you ask Him in My name. I am giving you these commands so that you may love one another."

What more does the Bible say about fruit? There are several kinds of fruit that will be clear in someone who is born again:

- Fruit of Repentance

"Bear fruit worthy of repentance." (Matthew 3:8) Repentance means turning away from a self-ruled life to a God-ruled life. The Bible says faith alone saves us, however there can be no faith in Christ without repentance and no repentance without faith. Ephesians 2:8-9, *"For by grace you have been saved through faith, and this is not your own doing; it is the gift of God, not the result of works, so that no one may boast."*

The fruit of repentance is seen when we realize we have offended the nature and character of our Lord and feel grief over it. We realize the majesty and holiness of God and hate anything that sets itself contrary to that. False repentance puts on a self-serving show when needed and doesn't produce lasting change. Genuine repentance (and the only kind the Lord receives) is grieved over anything that grieves the Lord, and the person changes through the power of Christ in him/her.

- Fruit of Good Works

> *"So that you may lead lives worthy of the Lord, fully pleasing to Him, as you bear fruit in every good work and as you grow in the knowledge of God."*
>
> Colossians 1:10

> *"I desire that you insist on these things, so that those who have come to believe in God may be careful*

> *to devote themselves to good works; these things*
> *are excellent and profitable to everyone."*
>
> Titus 3:8

John Wesley said, "Do all the good you can, by all the means you can, in all the ways you can, in all the places you can, to all the people you can, as long as you ever can." Although good works do not get us to heaven, they testify of our genuine faith. They are the fruit that people can see and know we are genuine.

- Fruit of Thanksgiving

> *"Through Him, then, let us continually offer a sacrifice of praise to God, that is, the fruit of lips that confess His name."*
>
> Hebrews 13:15

> *"As you therefore have received Christ Jesus the Lord, continue to live your lives in Him, rooted and built up in Him and established in the faith, just as you were taught, abounding in thanksgiving."*
>
> Colossians 2:6-7

- Fruit of the Spirit

> *"By contrast, the fruit of the Spirit is love, joy, peace, patience, kindness, generosity, faithfulness, gentleness and self-control. There is no law against such things. And those who belong to Christ Jesus have crucified the flesh with its passions and desires. If we live by the Spirit, let us also be guided by the Spirit."*
>
> Galatians 5:22-25

All this fruit produces a harvest of righteousness: *"Having produced the harvest of righteousness that comes through Jesus Christ for the glory and praise of God."* (Philippians 1:11)

We know what good fruit looks like and what it produces. Let's look at fruit the Bible warns is toxic:

> *"Now the practices of the sinful nature are clearly evident: they are sexual immorality, impurity, sensuality (total irresponsibility, lack of self-control), idolatry, sorcery, hostility, strife, jealousy, fits of anger, disputes, dissensions, factions [that promote heresies], envy, drunkenness, riotous behavior and other things like these. I warn you beforehand, just as I did previously, that those who practice such things will not inherit the kingdom of God."*
>
> Galatians 5:19-21 (AMP)

To summarize Barnes notes on this passage, the works of the flesh are corrupt, unrenewed, and made plain and well known. As you read this, can you see characteristics of abusers?

- Witchcraft is characterized by someone who tries to impose their will on others, which is rebellion against God.
- Hatred is a lack of love that produces contention and strife.
- Strife here is tied to Romans 1:29 which is someone being filled with all unrighteousness, wickedness, greed, evil, full of envy, murder, strife, deceit, malice, gossips.
- Emulations is ardor or zeal in a bad cause, leading to strife.
- Wrath here is tied to 2 Corinthians 12:20, strife, jealousy, angry tempers, disputes, slanders, gossip, arrogance, disturbances.
- Seditions is tied to Romans 16:17, *"Now I urge you, brethren,*

keep your eye on those who cause dissensions and hindrances contrary to the teaching which you learned, and turn away from them."

To quote Barnes about those who will NOT inherit the kingdom of God:

> Shall not inherit the kingdom of God - Cannot possibly be saved; see the notes at 1 Corinthians 6:9-11. In regard to this passage, we may remark:... this passage is full of fearful admonition to those who indulge in any or all of these vices. Paul, inspired of God, has solemnly declared, that such cannot be saved. They cannot enter into the kingdom of heaven as they are. Nor is it desirable that they should. What would heaven be if filled up with adulterers, and fornicators, and idolaters, with the proud and envious, and with murderers, and drunkards? To call such a place heaven, would be an abuse of the word. No one could wish to dwell there; and such people cannot enter into heaven.
>
> ... the human heart must be changed, or man cannot be saved. This follows of course. If such is its tendency, then there is a necessity for such a change as that in regeneration, in order that man may be happy and be saved... We should rejoice that such people cannot, with their present characters, be admitted to heaven...
>
> How cheering the thought that there is one world where these vices are unknown; one world, all whose ample plains may be traversed, and the note of blasphemy shall never fall on the ear; one world, where virtue shall be safe from the arts of the seducer; one world where we may forever dwell, and not one reeling and staggering drunkard shall ever be seen; where there shall be not one family in want and tears from the vice of its unfaithful head! (emphasis mine)With

what joy should we look forward to that world! With what ardor should we pant that it may be our own! (6)

These verses have identified unrepentant abusers among others of ungodly character. If God will not allow them in His home and will not live with them, then why would we ever assume that He demands it of us? God does not have a double standard and His opinion of those who deliberately cause pain to others is clear. He's not turning a blind eye to it and He's not afraid to call it what it is! We don't have to be afraid either.

> *"In fact when we call sin and hypocrisy what it is, we come into agreement with Him, a good and safe place to be. "What then shall we say to all these things? If God is for us, who can be [successful] against us?"*
>
> Romans 8:31 (AMP)

Another way to look at this is to read what the Bible says about fools and foolishness. One can replace the word "fool" with the word "abuser." The description is the same for both. An abusive husband is a fool and his fruit is toxic! Here are characteristics of fools found in the book of Proverbs:

- Fools don't learn from their mistakes but keep repeating them (26:11)
- They despise knowledge (1:22)
- Are quick-tempered (12:16)
- Deceitful (14:8)
- They don't want to understand, but rather to air their own opinions (18:2-3)
- They despise wisdom and discipline (1:5-7)
- They lie and manipulate (10:18-19)

- Doing wrong is fun for them (10:23-25)
- They will not make things right when they have hurt someone (14:8-10)
- They trust in themselves (28:26)
- They are hot-heads (29:11)
- They spend unwisely (21:20)
- They bring grief and bitterness to their family (17:25)
- They despise those who are wise (23:9)
- They are reckless and careless (14:16)

So what kind of fruit is your husband producing? Fruit of wisdom or fruit of foolishness? Fruit of righteousness or works of the flesh? If he is a Christian as he may claim, then he will grow, as we all should, in grace and love. It doesn't mean he won't make mistakes. We all do. But he will accept correction and instruction in living a biblical Christian life. Good character and integrity should dominate the flaws.

Religion produces some passionate though dangerously deluded people. If his actions don't line up with the Bible, then stop being manipulated with the title. Accept that it is bogus. Don't feel guilty for seeing and accepting the truth rather than the lies. When I no longer bought the line of "Christian" nonsense Brian fed me, he gave up on it.

Reflection: Thankfulness

Thankfulness. One good fruit mentioned is the fruit of thankfulness. The thankfulness that the Lord wants us to have is not limited to when things feel good or seem right. Complaining when things don't feel right is contrary to the peace that we are called to abide in.

John 15:5, *"I am the vine, you are the branches. Those who abide in me and I in them bear much fruit, because apart from me you can do nothing."* Our feelings are deceptive representations of reality and will lead us astray if allowed to dominate us.

It's easy to experience gratitude when we are pleased with the way something is going. But what happens when people are doing things that hurt us or we're faced with circumstances that are painful or challenging? By maintaining a thankful heart, we are open to receive healing and see possibility and solutions.

A few benefits of intentional thankfulness are:

- Greater optimism and a more positive outlook
- Higher energy levels and more relaxation
- Increased resilience to trauma and stress
- Reducing black and white, hopeless thinking
- Makes us future and solution-oriented
- Better sleep

Enough quality sleep can reduce anxiety, depression, pain and stress. It also boosts our immune system which makes us healthier overall. What is one thing you can do to create a more restful sleeping environment?

- Who has helped you become the person you are today? What's the top thing you'd thank them for?
- What's something that inspired you recently?
- What is something non-physical you have received lately, such as time, kindness, a smile, support?
- What valuable life-lesson have you learned recently?
- Have you experienced any blessings in disguise lately?

- If something didn't go the way you hoped, can you identify something good from it that's worth having?
- What choices have you made in the last five years you're thankful for?
- What's something you're looking forward to?
- Who in your life has survived something difficult and overcome?
- Have you recently imagined a worst-case scenario that didn't happen?

Tips for Cultivating Gratitude

- First, recognize the goodness you have in your life. Use the questions above to get started.
- Second, recognize the source of that goodness that lies outside of yourself. Psalm 16:2 reads: *"I say to the Lord, 'You are my Lord; I have no good apart from you.'"*
- Take time today to come up with a gratitude list. It's especially beneficial to think over before you get out of bed in the morning. If it doesn't come easily, don't let that stop you from still giving thanks.

Use these prompts to get started:

- I'm thankful for my family because…
- Something good that happened this week is…
- I am grateful for my friendship with… because…
- I'm grateful for who I am because…
- Something silly I am grateful for is…
- Something else I am grateful for is…

"Cultivate the habit of being grateful for every good thing that comes to you, and to give thanks continuously. And because all things have contributed to your advancement, you should include all things in your gratitude."

~ Ralph Waldo Emerson

Foundation

"Rejoice always and delight in your faith; be unceasing and persistent in prayer; in every situation [no matter what the circumstances] be thankful and continually give thanks to God; for this is the will of God for you in Christ Jesus."

1 Thessalonians 5:16-18 (AMP)

"Let the [spoken] word of Christ have its home within you [dwelling in your heart and mind—permeating every aspect of your being] as you teach [spiritual things] and admonish and train one another with all wisdom, singing psalms and hymns and spiritual songs with thankfulness in your hearts to God. Whatever you do [no matter what it is] in word or deed, do everything in the name of the Lord Jesus [and in dependence on Him], giving thanks to God the Father through Him."

Colossians 3:16-17 (AMP)

"Those who bring thanksgiving as their sacrifice honor me; to those who go the right way I will show the salvation of God."

Psalm 50:23

Chapter 9

Don't You Dare Judge Me!

HAVE YOU EVER had Matthew 7:1 thrown in your face whenever you questioned someone's beliefs or behavior? (*"Do not judge, so you may not be judged."*) Pastor David Curtis at *The Berean Bible Church* has an excellent teaching that clarifies the real meaning of it:

> Many people have misunderstood Jesus' admonition concerning judging. When Jesus says that we are not to judge, many people have interpreted that to mean that we are not to engage in any form of analysis or evaluation of others. In other words, this line of thinking says that we cannot conclude that a person's behavior or lifestyle is wrong, and that they are consequently wrong for engaging in it. Those who would like to justify all manner of evil use this verse to chasten anyone who would take a stand for righteousness.
>
> This verse is also misused when referring to other people's religious beliefs. Some people seem to say that we must sacrifice our ability to discriminate in decision making. Such a position would require that we exercise no discernment.

There is a sense in which we are not to judge people, but we will see in this study that there is a sense in which we, as believers, are required to judge others. (7)

There are many verses that command us to judge righteous judgment:

- Matthew 7:15-16 commands us to test who is a true and false prophet
- 1 John 4:1-2 tells us to test the spirits to see if they are of God
- 1 Corinthians 10:15 says to judge what is being said as in weighing and forming an opinion or consideration
- 2 Thessalonians 3:6 commands us to withdraw from people who walk disorderly
- Romans 16:17 tells us to avoid people who cause division and offense
- 1 Corinthians 5:6-7 says to purge out the "old leaven"

There are several more verses, but these show we have to use judgment with others. Pastor David also shares three attitudes that comprise righteous judgment:

> First, we are not to have a self-righteous judgmental attitude. Philippians 2:3 says *"Do nothing from selfish ambition or conceit, but in humility regard others as better than yourselves."*
>
> Secondly, we are not to judge the motives of others. We should not attempt to become the judge of another person's thoughts, the motives of their heart, or attempt to enter into the court of their conscience. Jeremiah 17:10 says *"I the Lord test the mind and search the heart, to give to all according to their ways, according to the fruit of their doings."*
>
> Thirdly, we are not to judge hypocritically. The one who is

quick to detect the minor faults of others while blind to, or unconcerned about, their own serious sins is a hypocrite. Matthew 7:3-5 says, *"Why do you see the speck in your neighbor's eye, but do not notice the log in your own eye? 4 Or how can you say to your neighbor, 'Let me take the speck out of your eye,' while the log is in your own eye? 5 You hypocrite, first take the log out of your own eye, and then you will see clearly to take the speck out of your neighbor's eye."* A "hypocrite" is the actor of a part, one pretending to be very zealous as to the requirements of holiness, while himself living in neglect and great sin... be faithful in dealing with yourself, unsparingly judging yourself before God, putting away out of your heart and life whatsoever you know to be displeasing unto God. (8)

I hope this helps relieve you of guilt you have been carrying over seeing and questioning things you suspect are not right. God wants you to do that! God has given His children discernment to make us aware and protect us from those who would cause us harm. Keep your heart clear with God and thank Him every time He helps you to see through pretension and deception. On that note, use your discernment when you hear testimonies…

I didn't find out the biblical truth about headship and submission until after I left Brian. Had I understood it earlier, I would have gotten the girls and myself out quicker. In the meantime, as I struggled to hold things together, I leaned on the certainty that Brian's testimony was real and his abusiveness was just a passing phase. I hoped that he was a good guy who just needed a supportive wife and time to work through some things and then everything would be okay.

I grew up reading books and hearing on television or at church testimonials about bad people turned good after accepting Christ into their hearts. Drug addicts and alcoholics delivered from addictions. Criminals walking away from a life of crime. Broken relationships restored. Sexual trauma healed. The list is long, and I am NOT saying God doesn't save, heal and deliver. He does! I am saying that there are fraudulent testimonies used to manipulate people and your husband's might be one.

Brian's testimony was one of the most dramatic I had heard. He claimed in prison God brought him instant deliverance from a long life of hard-core drug abuse and dealing, prostitution, violence, gangs and other serious criminal behavior.

When I met him, his testimony seemed genuine and glorifying to God. Instant deliverance from deplorable lifelong behavior that had begun as a young boy? Sure! God can do anything! Brian even claimed a miraculous healing from an STD, verified by the prison doctor.

Brian seemed thrilled to be set free from his former life, learned the Bible inside out while in prison, preached to other inmates when he could, and believed God had called him to be a preacher to the world. Everything was so spiritual and appeared valid. I guess I wouldn't have known what invalid looked like though since I didn't even consider testimonies could be false.

I was naïve and trusting, one of the main reasons abusers, con artists and predators target Christians. My marriage to Brian was a rude awakening to phony testimonies. Brian kept this facade of devout Christianity for the first three years of our marriage. When he gave it up, I still clung to it. Except for isolated incidents, Brian stopped pretending to be a Christian. He went back to drinking and drugging and was furious with God for not making him a preacher.

Brian's actions, words and reasoning were so conflicting, that I often felt off balance and like I was going a little crazy. Add to it that "Paul" stayed in the mix and I retreated within myself. I stayed focused on my daughters and tried to not go crazy with Brian's world. At least he continued to work, provide and was not physically violent, so I figured everything would work out. It didn't.

I now have a healthy caution toward people who claim to be radically saved and changed overnight. Again, I am NOT saying God doesn't deliver in amazing ways. But it is foolish to accept every testimony offered at face value. Christianity is a favorite escape for people who need to hide and want to prey on trusting and generous people.

I have found in the years since, that though God performs miracles, a person's core character does not change overnight. Instantaneous change of character is rare. While a drug addict may be delivered from his addiction at a prayer meeting, it takes time and effort for his habits and ingrained way of thinking to change for the long term.

If what he claims is just for show, he can pretend for a long time if he has strong willpower. However, the truth will come out. TIME and FRUIT are the precious qualifiers of what is genuine and what is false. In the years I have helped victims of domestic abuse and violence, it is sickening how often the abuser claims to be a Christian, and is a pastor, church leader or otherwise active in church.

I held on to Brian's original testimony for dear life, thinking the setback was temporary and he needed me to pray him through a rough time. I was so blind. He knew it too. He took full advantage of my trust, naivety and spiritual faith. My plea to you is to not disregard bad behavior because he has given you a spiritual testimony. Anyone can do that.

Pastor Jeff Crippen compares a man with a false testimony to a fool in Proverbs in his message *You Cannot Drive Abuse Out of the Abuser*:

> *"Crush a fool in a mortar with a pestle along with crushed grain, yet his folly will not depart from him."* (Proverbs 27:22) The

fool in Proverbs is not merely some simple-minded person. Nope. This fool is a wicked individual. You can check this out for yourself if you want by simply reading the occurrences of "fool" in this book of Holy Scripture. And many of the descriptions of this fool given us by Solomon describe the abuser we know so well perfectly.

So, look at this verse cited above. What does it tell us about the fool/abuser? It says that you can sooner grind him up in a flour-making machine (a mortar and pestle in those days) and get his blood out than you can use even the most severe methods on him to "bleed him" dry of his abuse. Which is all to say this: you can't fix an abuser... Not this guy who so often claims to be a Christian, but whose very essence of personhood is a profound sense of entitlement to power and control and who feels quite justified in using whatever evil tactics he needs to employ to get what he wants. You can't fix him. That is what these divinely inspired and inerrant words are telling us.

Too many people, this fact seems disturbing. I mean, can't Christ change anyone? Aren't we as Christians supposed to "have faith" in the Lord's ability to give anyone a new heart and do whatever we can to lead such people to salvation in Christ? Christ gives a new heart to anyone who calls upon Him in real faith and repentance. But abusers don't do so. For all their common claims that they have changed, that they have really repented, for all the crocodile tears they shed, they do not humbly come to Christ in genuine faith, exercising real repentance. Crush them, winnow them, sift them all you like, their folly is not going to depart from them.

This seems disturbing to many people, but I find it a source of the very beginning of freedom from abuse. When an abuse victim comes to clearly understand that not only is her abuser an abuser, but that there is nothing she can do to change him by driving his abusive mentality out of him, then she can begin to take steps to get free. (9)

How does your husband's behavior make you feel? Does it make you feel loved, cared about, secure and happy? Or does it make you feel anxious, worthless, crazy or depressed? Your feelings are a major indicator that his behavior is toxic or not. That applies to anyone in your life. You don't have to understand why to know the truth. Pay attention to how his behavior makes you feel. If you are feeling bad, then something is wrong with it and warrants further investigation.

Honor your gut instincts. If you have been shutting them down, start by acknowledging them to God when they come up: *"Lord, I am feeling _____ right now. Something isn't right. Thank you for protecting my children and me, and for helping me to see truth. As truth is revealed, give me the wisdom and strength to know how to respond to it."*

I trust that by now you have determined if you are in a toxic, abusive relationship. Hopefully Scripture has cleared up any confusion you had about the genuineness of your husband's claim of faith in God and Christian tenants.

In the next chapter, we will lay the foundation for interpreting what Scripture says about his headship and your submission.

Reflection: Discernment

Discernment. It is the ability to decide between truth and error, right and wrong. Discernment is a "knowing" that can sometimes feel similar to a gut instinct, but it does not originate with us.

God has given you a storehouse of inner wisdom. James 1:5, *"If any of you is lacking in wisdom, ask God, who gives to all generously and ungrudgingly, and it will be given you."* With this wisdom and discernment you have all the answers you need to live your life with purpose and minimal mistakes. Without it is like being a boat tossed around by life's experiences and no rudder to get to where you want to be. Discernment is your rudder. It puts you back in control.

Failure to recognize or acknowledge red flags leads to believing things that are not true and being susceptible to manipulation. The key to living a life that is fulfilling and joyful lies in your ability to exercise discernment in every area of life.

When you face a decision, use these questions to gain clarity:

- Am I being pressured to make this decision quickly before I have time to think on it?
- Would this choice propel me toward an inspiring future or keep me stuck in past patterns?
- Is this choice an act of faith, fear or denial?
- Does this choice increase my integrity?
- Which option gives me an 'aha' feeling and creates positive feelings?
- Which choice leads to bleaker feelings or a sense of pointlessness?
- Does this choice require that I change sabotaging patterns?
- Am I willing to pause and get feedback from people whose judgment and wisdom I trust?
- If I feel discomfort, is it because the choice will stretch and grow me positively?

Tips for Accessing Discernment

- Start with what you know. Lay out all the facts to consider before venturing into the unknown.

- Let go of your need for others approval. Ask yourself, is this right for me? Does this resonate with me or am I saying yes when I want to say no?

- Know your core values. Which choice honors them? Which choice negates them?

- Talk to at least one person you respect and ask for their advice.

- Get quiet. Make time to be alone with your thoughts and inner wisdom.

- Invite God to speak to you. This may be through thoughts, feelings and memories He stirs within you to guide you. There may be a scripture that comes to mind that sheds light on the situation or confirms the choice you are considering. Remember He has a good plan for you in His perfect love.

- Check out the fruit (outcome) of your potential choice. Is there peace? Or confusion and ickiness?

- Wait if you can before deciding. We often make mistakes when we jump into something quickly.

- Commit and go for it, knowing you did the best you could to make the right choice. Put it in the Lord's hands and go forth in faith!

Foundation

"And this I pray, that your love may abound still more and more in real knowledge and all discernment."

Philippians 1:9 (NASB)

*In other translations of Philippians 1:9, as sited above, the word discernment is used interchangeably with the words judgment, profound insight, perception and understanding. It also means "to see into," "have knowledge," or "detect."

"But examine everything carefully; hold fast to that which is good; abstain from every form of evil."

1 Thessalonians 5:21-22 (NASB)

"But solid food is for the mature, whose spiritual senses perceive heavenly matters. And they have been adequately trained by what they've experienced to emerge with understanding of the difference between what is truly excellent and what is evil and harmful."

Hebrews 5:14 (TPT)

"And let the peace of Christ rule in your hearts, to which indeed you were called in the one body. And be thankful."

Colossians 3:15

Chapter 10

How to Interpret Scripture

AS A DEVOTED Christian wife and mother in an abusive marriage, I suffered with guilt, confusion and fear as I tried everything in my power to save our marriage. I tried to do this under a religious belief system that undermined my desire to be happy and raise my children in a healthy environment.

I felt in my heart that demanding absolute submission of me with no way out was wrong. It did not agree with the character of the God whom I loved and followed. However, my religious beliefs were so ingrained that I couldn't wrap my mind around something different.

I desperately wanted to see the truth in the Bible. I wanted to ease the guilt that plagued me for not just accepting that the abuse wasn't worse. Try harder... Pray more... Be more submissive... Be more understanding... Be more enthusiastic in the bedroom... I hated it!

As traditional theology had taught me, physical adultery, abandonment or death was the only way out of a marriage. Since Brian was very much alive and wasn't leaving me, and I couldn't verify an affair, it appeared I was condemned to live with the abuse.

However, God answers every heart's cry for truth! It has taken time for me to receive the glorious truth about what God (not man) says about headship and submission. It is simple and full of hope for you. I share it, trusting that His simple yet powerful truths will set you free as they did me.

In Isaiah 1:18, God is heartbroken over His people's rebellion and corruption and He calls out to them: *"Come now, let us argue it out..."* (to prove, decide, judge, rebuke, reprove, correct and be right)

Ephesians 5:17 admonishes us to understand God's will: *"So do not be foolish, but understand what the will of the Lord is."*

It may be hard to accept that what you believe about your marriage and God may be distorted. God wants us to examine and question things. He never asks us to take what anyone says about Him at face value and structure our lives around it. We are thinking beings in a world full of fallacy and error. We please God when we take things to Him and examine the veracity.

When my eyes opened to the fact that many of my beliefs were wrong and the source of unnecessary heartache, it relieved me to discover the truth. It took time though for it to make sense and my thinking to change. Satan does not want you to know the truth because it will set you and your children free from bondage and destruction.

God wants you to know what is true and right so you can make good choices and live in the light and freedom of His love and care. He has given us guidelines to help us know what to do about the difficult situations we find ourselves in. There is an answer and hope!

Let's keep in mind biblical principles as we question what we have been taught about headship and submission. The Bible will reinforce what we believe, or reprove and correct thinking that is in error. My goal is not to tell you what to do, but to arm you with knowledge so you can make the best decisions for yourself and your family. It starts with reading the Bible for yourself.

Why You Should Read the Bible for Yourself

It is life

> *"It is the spirit that gives life; the flesh is useless. The words that I have spoken to you are spirit and life."*
>
> John 6:63

> *"But first and most importantly seek (aim at, strive after) His kingdom and His righteousness [His way of doing and being right—the attitude and character of God], and all these things will be given to you also."*
>
> Matthew 6:33 (AMP)

Jesus is saying that if we put Him first, everything else will come into proper place and priority in our lives. God's kingdom is the rule and reign of Jesus Christ in the personal lives of those who are spiritually born again. His righteousness means we are in right-relationship with Him, or we are giving top priority to cooperating with Him.

"All these things will be given to you" reflects Philippians 4:19, *"And my God will fully satisfy every need of yours according to his riches in glory in Christ Jesus."* Now, our idea of what we need often differs from God's. But God wants us to rest in His love, knowing He will care for us in His wisdom and sovereignty. He is the giver of life!

It brings wisdom

"Do not forsake her, and she will keep you; love her, and she will guard you. The beginning of wisdom is this: Get wisdom, and whatever else you get, get insight. Prize her highly, and she will exalt you; she will honor you if you embrace her. She will place on your head a fair garland; she will bestow on you a beautiful crown. Hear, my child, and accept my words, that the years of your life may be many. I have taught you the way of wisdom; I have led you in the paths of uprightness. When you walk, your step will not be hampered; and if you run, you will not stumble."

Proverbs 4:6-12

Who of us doesn't want wisdom? Especially when we are in a toxic relationship and don't know what to do. Jesus has the answer for every question we have. Seek for it and it will come. You may have several conflicting sources of information and advice coming at you, causing uncertainty and fear. The best thing I did was to take all these things to God and confess I didn't have a clue what to do, and worse of all, I was too scared to do anything, but too scared not to do anything!

I can't say God ever wrote on the wall telling me precisely what I should do. However, in hindsight, I can see He led me. He gave me wisdom. He guided my choices. Much of it I had to do in faith, never certain if I was doing the right thing or not.

God honored my asking Him for wisdom and direction. My faith that He answered my prayer pleased Him. In the end, everything worked out. I made mistakes along the way, but when I realized it, I went back to the Lord and asked for help. He ALWAYS helped me through everything. Not once did He ever fail my daughters or me. Not once did He ever fail to fulfill His Word in our lives. He will do the same for you too.

Speaking of mistakes, in hindsight, I also see I made those when I was acting out of fear and haste. This leads to the next great reason for reading the Bible…

It brings peace

> *"Peace I leave with you; My [perfect] peace I give to you; not as the world gives do I give to you. Do not let your heart be troubled, nor let it be afraid. [Let My perfect peace calm you in every circumstance and give you courage and strength for every challenge.]"*
>
> John 14:27 (AMP)

> *"Do not worry about anything, but in everything by prayer and supplication with thanksgiving let your requests be made known to God. And the peace of God, which surpasses all understanding, will guard your hearts and your minds in Christ Jesus."*
>
> Philippians 4:6-7

When we study the topic of peace, we receive great comfort and courage during conflict and turmoil. As I mentioned earlier, I made mistakes when I took matters into my own hands out of fear and being in a hurry. As long as I abided in a peaceful state of mind and heart, somehow things would work out. Urgent issues would often resolve themselves. When I became afraid and reacted things didn't go so well. I would encourage you to do a Bible study on peace. It will change your outlook and your life!

Six Principles for Discernment

God is the ultimate source of authority

"All scripture is inspired by God and is useful for teaching, for reproof, for correction, and for training in righteousness, so that everyone who belongs to God may be proficient, equipped for every good work."

2 Timothy 3:16-17

"For thus says the Lord, who created the heavens (He is God!), who formed the earth and made it (He established it; He did not create it a chaos, He formed it to be inhabited!): I am the Lord, and there is no other."

Isaiah 45:18

"For by Him all things were created in heaven and on earth, [things] visible and invisible, whether thrones or dominions or rulers or authorities; all things were created and exist through Him [that is, by His activity] and for Him. And He Himself existed and is before all things, and in Him all things hold together. [His is the controlling, cohesive force of the universe.]"

Colossians 1:16-17 (AMP)

When there is a conflict between our belief and God's Word, then we must side with God. Contemporary culture is producing many non-biblical or extra-biblical teachings and practices. Whatever error it is, it results from misinterpreting the Bible. You may feel it is confusing to know the difference, but it isn't if you understand the principles of interpreting the Bible. God wants us to understand. Satan is the author of confusion and distortion, not God.

God knows your past, your future, and He knows your heart and that of everyone around you. You can be open and honest with Him about your questions, fears, confusion and everything else. He knows it anyway, and when you are transparent before Him you honor Him. Better to make mistakes in His presence rather than away from Him! Make Him the authority in your life now, where you are, as you are. You will never regret it.

God will never reveal or speak something that contradicts the Bible

Many modern questionable "Christian" practices and teachings are justified by one verse, that God is doing *"a new thing."* (Isaiah 42:9) Has God turned His back on His Word and decided to do something new and out of character? Never! Do you see the modern church and Christians representing Jesus? Are we the spotless bride of Christ? Or do you see a sick, defiled and corrupt body ruled by selfishness, apathy and compromise? Is God going to abandon us and raise up a new bride? No!

God will draw us back to Himself. He will deliver us from a shallow frivolous gospel that has led us astray. He will destroy every false gospel and put to shame every false teacher and prophet.

> *"I will lead the blind by a road they do not know, by paths they have not known I will guide them. I will turn the darkness before them into light, the rough places into level ground. These are the things I will do, and I will not forsake them."*
>
> Isaiah 42:16

Friend, THAT is the "new thing" we can look forward to! Our darkness will become light. The rough places smoothed. God will purify us as His bride and restore us back to what He always intended us to be.

Feelings, experiences, visions, prophesies and doctrines must always agree with God's written Word. If it does not, then the Bible says to reject it:

> *"I urge you, brothers and sisters, to keep your eyes on those who cause dissensions and create obstacles or introduce temptations [for others] to commit sin, [acting in ways] contrary to the doctrine which you have learned. Turn away from them."*
>
> Romans 16:17 (AMP)

Things have to line up with God's nature and character

By reading the Bible for ourselves, we get to know the revealed nature and character of God, such as God is sovereign, living and true. He is life and the source of all life. He is eternal. God is loving, just and fair. He is merciful and good. He is truthful and faithful. God wants to heal, restore, reconcile, deliver and set people free from bondage.

God also feels emotion. When you grieve, He grieves. When you rejoice, He rejoices with you. He walks with you through the ups and downs of life.

> *"Blessed [gratefully praised and adored] be the God and Father of our Lord Jesus Christ, the Father of mercies and the God of all comfort, who comforts and encourages us in every trouble so that we will be able to comfort and encourage those who are in any kind of trouble, with the comfort with which we ourselves are comforted by God."*
>
> 2 Corinthians 1:3-4 (AMP)

> *"He was despised and rejected by men, A Man of sorrows and pain and acquainted with grief; And like One from whom men hide their faces He was despised, and we did not appreciate His worth or esteem Him."*
>
> Isaiah 53:3 (AMP)

Test all teaching for sound doctrine, and test all lives for the fruit of the Spirit

> *"Beloved, do not believe every spirit, but test the spirits to see whether they are from God; for many false prophets have gone out into the world."*
>
> 1 John 4:1

How do we test the spirits? By comparing what is being taught to Scripture and evaluating if the person is living in the fruit of the Spirit. We should also test our own words and actions to be sure we are in truth. (Galatians 6:4)

> *"How much are we supposed to test? Everything. "But test all things carefully [so you can recognize what is good]. Hold firmly to that which is good."*
>
> 1 Thessalonians 5:21

By reading the Bible for yourself, you will know if what someone tells you stands the test of Scripture. No prophet, husband or pastor has the freedom to reinvent God's Word. The Bible will stand strong through time—it will never fail us. It is a rock that will keep us safe in turbulent times. God will defend His Word and your choice to follow Him. Reading from your Bible every day and conversing with

Him builds a relationship that will carry you through difficult times, difficult relationships and opposition.

Take into consideration the historical, cultural and literary background

The University of St. Thomas has an informative section on biblical exegesis. Part of that is examining the background of the writer and the context:

> What can be known of the historical situation prior to and during the time the biblical book was written? How did society function at that time, e.g., what was the status of women, children or slaves in the culture, what religions existed at the time of writing, or what were the main cultural values in society? What other texts might be like the book that contains your passage from the same time period? Are there other texts that might help you understand your passage? The Bible did not float down from heaven untouched by human hands. Rather, it was written over a long period of time, by real people. Who lived in real homes, with real families in real cultures. (10)

Last, but not least, you are not inferior because you are a woman

> *"There is [now no distinction in regard to salvation] neither Jew nor Greek, there is neither slave nor free, there is neither male nor female; for you [who believe] are all one in Christ Jesus [no one can claim a spiritual superiority]."*
>
> Galatians 3:28 (AMP)

I want to close with what Kyle Butt, M.Div. clarifies the actual biblical view of women is in contrast to popular opinion:

The militant skeptical community incessantly attempts to discredit the Bible and the God Who is represented in its pages. One line of reasoning used in their efforts is to demand that the Bible presents a sexist picture of men and women, in which God and the Bible writers place more value on men, and view women as inferior and of less inherent worth. This accusation falls apart, however, when the entirety of the text is considered. Careful study reveals that Bible writers personified and illustrated such invaluable attributes as wisdom in the form of a woman. God himself compares traits that He possesses to similar traits found in women. Both the Old and New Testaments are filled with narratives lauding the actions of faithful, powerful women.

The apostle Paul, who is often accused of misogyny, makes one of the boldest statements of gender equality ever recorded in religious literature. And the misguided attempt to discredit Paul by claiming that different gender roles in his epistles prove he valued women less cannot honestly or reasonably be sustained. In truth, the Bible presents the clearest picture of gender equity, value and inherent worth ever recorded in either ancient or modern literature. The status of women in the Holy Scriptures, not only is not a challenge to its divine inspiration, but the biblical treatment of women actually provides another piece of evidence for the Bible's perfection and inspiration. (11)

Now we have built a biblical foundation for interpreting the Word of God. We will examine in the next chapter what it says about headship and submission.

Reflection: Intellectual Independence

Intellectual independence. Are you able to think for yourself? Or are your thoughts shaped by others—spouse, parents, clergy, society, the media? When you don't think for yourself, you give up control and the ability to decide what's best for your life. Other people can manipulate you into believing, not what benefits you, but what benefits them.

Thinking for yourself doesn't mean knowing everything or checking every fact. It means resisting passiveness and exerting the effort to learn and think outside your comfort zone. It also means to feed your mind from a variety of sources that may challenge your accepted beliefs.

Abusive and dysfunctional relationships depend on unquestioned authority and blind conformity to survive. Do you tell yourself that you are not worthy of anything better; that you can't survive without your spouse; that you deserve to be battered and abused; that it is all your fault; that it's too late to change anything; that you need to submit and pray more and everything will be okay?

Such beliefs keep you in a dysfunctional relationship. But you can examine these beliefs and challenge their veracity. You do that by reading this book and being open to learning something new, even if it's uncomfortable.

In a healthy relationship, both partners appreciate and support critical thinking. If your spouse gets angry when you question him or resist his ideas, you are in a toxic relationship. In a healthy relationship, partners exchange ideas and discuss things from different angles. Each one makes the other one better, as Proverbs 27:17 puts it, *"iron sharpens iron, and one person sharpens the wits of another."*

You are NOT thinking for yourself when:

- You let others talk or pressure you into something that is not right for you
- You passively go along with whatever…
- You accept stereotypes based on sex, race or culture
- You do or believe something just because it's always been that way
- You accept something without questioning the validity

Critical thinking is thinking on purpose! The following questions will help you exercise your critical thinking muscle:

- What evidence can you present for/against …?
- Does … really make sense?
- What are the advantages and disadvantages of …?
- What is the fruit of …?
- How can you judge the accuracy of …?
- Who benefits from …?
- What might be a hidden agenda behind …?
- How is … related to …?
- What ideas could you add to … and how would these ideas change it?
- What patterns do you notice in …?

Tips for Critical Thinking

Thinking for yourself is a skill that must be practiced and nurtured:

- Set aside emotion and use reason to evaluate
- Consider other perspectives
- Maintain an open mind

- Be willing to change your mind
- Consider other reasonable possibilities
- Be aware of cognitive distortions affecting your beliefs and thinking

Foundation

"A gullible person will believe anything, but a sensible person will confirm the facts."

Proverbs 14:15 (TPT)

"Do not forsake her [wisdom], and she will keep you; love her, and she will guard you. The beginning of wisdom is this: Get wisdom, and whatever else you get, get insight."

Proverbs 4:6-7

"If any of you is lacking in wisdom, ask God, who gives to all generously and ungrudgingly, and it will be given you."

James 1:5

Chapter 11

Headship and Submission

"Male headship sets the stage for domestic violence. I don't subscribe to that in any way, shape, or form. When we talk about a man and a woman in the sacrament of matrimony, we're talking about a partnership, people working together. One partner is just as much the expression of God's creation as the other."

~ Father Michael McDermott

LET'S LOOK AT some scriptures used to enforce marital control and submission, and how a growing number of theologians interpret them. When I first discovered these truths, I felt like I had found a priceless treasure! Finally, the Word of God was lining up with the nature and character I knew of Him—a God of love, compassion and concern. The Bible made so much more sense and my relationship with God budded and grew like an eager new plant.

None of this is new. It has been God's intention all along. But my understanding of it was new. The old lies I believed dropped away, bringing me freedom, peace and joy. This is not an exhaustive study but a different perspective from respected theologians and leaders you may not have been exposed to before. Take what you learn here, study it further, and allow this to start a conversation between you and God.

First, I wrote out all the verses referred to, followed by the interpretations. Unless otherwise noted, I use the New Revised Standard Version, although the people I quote may use a different version.

> *"For the wife does not have authority over her own body, but the husband does; likewise the husband does not have authority over his own body, but the wife does."*
>
> 1 Corinthians 7:4

> *"For the Lord's sake accept the authority of every human institution, whether of the emperor as supreme…"*
>
> 1 Peter 2:13

> *"Wives, in the same way, accept the authority of your husbands, so that, even if some of them do not obey the word, they may be won over without a word by their wives' conduct, when they see the purity and reverence of your lives. Do not adorn yourselves outwardly by braiding your hair, and by wearing gold ornaments or fine clothing; rather, let your adornment be the inner self with the lasting beauty of a gentle and quiet spirit, which is very precious in God's sight. It was in this way long ago that the holy women who hoped in God used to adorn themselves by accepting the authority of their husbands. Thus Sarah obeyed Abraham and called him lord. You have become her daughters as long as you do what is good and never let fears alarm you. Husbands, in the same way, show consideration for*

your wives in your life together, paying honor to the woman as the weaker sex, since they too are also heirs of the gracious gift of life—so that nothing may hinder your prayers."

1 Peter 3:1-7

"Husbands, love your wives and never treat them harshly."

Colossians 3:19

"I therefore, the prisoner in the Lord, beg you to lead a life worthy of the calling to which you have been called, with all humility and gentleness, with patience, bearing with one another in love, making every effort to maintain the unity of the Spirit in the bond of peace."

Ephesians 4:1-3

"Be subject to one another out of reverence for Christ. Wives, be subject to your husbands as you are to the Lord. For the husband is the head of the wife just as Christ is the head of the church, the body of which He is the Savior. Just as the church is subject to Christ, so also wives ought to be, in everything, to their husbands. Husbands, love your wives, just as Christ loved the church and gave himself up for her, in order to make her holy by cleansing her with the washing of water by the word, so as to present the church to himself in splendor, without a spot or wrinkle or anything of the kind—yes, so that she may be holy and without blemish. In the same way, husbands should love their wives as they do their own bodies. He who loves his wife loves himself. For no one ever hates his own body, but he nourishes and tenderly cares for it, just as Christ does for the church, because we are

members of his body. 'For this reason a man will leave his father and mother and be joined to his wife, and the two will become one flesh.' This is a great mystery, and I am applying it to Christ and the church. Each of you, however, should love his wife as himself, and a wife should respect her husband."

Ephesians 5:21-33

"Mortal, prophesy against the shepherds of Israel: prophesy, and say to them—to the shepherds: Thus says the Lord God: Ah, you shepherds of Israel who have been feeding yourselves! Should not shepherds feed the sheep? You eat the fat, you clothe yourselves with the wool, you slaughter the fatlings; but you do not feed the sheep. You have not strengthened the weak, you have not healed the sick, you have not bound up the injured, you have not brought back the strayed, you have not sought the lost, but with force and harshness you have ruled them."

Ezekiel 34:2-4

"Submit yourselves therefore to God. Resist the devil, and he will flee from you."

James 4:7

"Woe to the shepherds who destroy and scatter the sheep of my pasture! says the LORD. Therefore thus says the LORD, the God of Israel, concerning the shepherds who shepherd my people: It is you who have scattered my flock, and have driven them away, and you have not attended to them. So I will attend to you for your evil doings, says the LORD. Then I myself will gather the remnant of my flock out of all the lands where I have driven them, and I will bring them back to their fold, and they shall

be fruitful and multiply. I will raise up shepherds over them who will shepherd them, and they shall not fear any longer, or be dismayed, nor shall any be missing, says the LORD."

Jeremiah 23:1-4

"So Jesus called them and said to them, 'You know that among the Gentiles those whom they recognize as their rulers lord it over them, and their great ones are tyrants over them. But it is not so among you; but whoever wishes to become great among you must be your servant, and whoever wishes to be first among you must be slave of all. For the Son of Man came not to be served but to serve, and to give his life a ransom for many.'"

Mark 10:42-45

Let's start with how Rev. Dr. Marie Fortune interprets headship and submission passages in her book, *Keeping the Faith: Questions and Answers for the Abused Woman*:

Question: The Bible says that the wife must submit to her husband. Does this mean that I must submit to his abuse?

Actually, the scriptural passage that refers to the husband-wife relationship begins by saying: *"Be subject to one another out of reverence for Christ."* (Ephesians 5:21) This is the starting point for all our relationships as Christians, inside the family or outside. Here the words "be subject to" also mean "accommodate to" or "give way to." This means that we should all, including husbands and wives, seek to be flexible with each other and give way to each other.

In another passage we find further clarification: *"Let each of you look not only to his own interests, but also to the interests* of others." (Philippians 2:4) So we are all, regardless of our relationship to each other, to be concerned for the other's welfare as well as for our own.

Then scripture proceeds to a specific reference to husbands and wives: *"Wives, be subject to your husbands, as to the Lord. For the husband is the head of the wife as Christ is the head of the church, his body, and is himself its Savior."* (Ephesians 5:22-23) This means that there are times in a Christian marriage when a wife should give way to her husband and recognize his interests as well as her own. But the husband's headship suggested here does not mean a role of unquestioned authority to which you are to be blindly obedient. What is described here is a model based on Christ's relationship to the church: Jesus was the servant of all who followed Him, and He gave Himself up for them. Never did He order people around, threaten, hit, or frighten them.

Almost all the rest of this passage from Ephesians spells out the instructions to the husband in his treatment of his wife: he is to be to her as Christ was to the church. This means he is to serve her needs and be willing to sacrifice himself for her if need be. This is what Jesus did for the church. He is to love his wife as himself, to nourish and cherish her. Another passage is even more specific: *"Husbands, love your wives, and do not be harsh with them."* (Colossians 3:19)

Clearly, the emphasis Scripture places on instructing husbands to care for and respect their wives just as Christ did the church leaves no room for excusing a husband's violent and abusive behavior toward his wife. (12)

ALL believers are called to mutual respect and submission to each other, *especially* husbands and wives. Paul, by using the example of the relationship between Christ and the church, dispels warped ideas of each partner's role in marriage. No tyrannical husband can claim to be living a Christian marriage. There is no justification for anything less than kindness, respect and sacrificial love for each other.

Jesus wasn't married, but if He was, can you picture Him treating His wife as your husband treats you? Jesus is our perfect example and He would never hurt or dominate you. Your husband has no biblical justification for doing it either.

Dr. Steven Tracy Ph.D., Professor of Theology and Ethics at Phoenix Seminary, says the submission passage in Ephesians focuses on the behavior of husbands rather than wives:

> It is tragically ironic that Paul's submission command to wives in Ephesians 5:24 has often been used against wives to condone or justify harsh and abusive behavior by husbands. The focus in this paragraph (quantitatively and qualitatively) is overwhelmingly on husbands. In Ephesians 5:21-33, Paul uses a mere forty-seven words to admonish wives, but one hundred and forty-three words to admonish husbands. Even more importantly, Paul raises the bar for husbands as high as it could possibly be raised by commanding them to love their wives as Christ loved the church and gave himself for her. This is surely the loftiest, most demanding command given to husbands in the entire Bible.
>
> But Paul does not leave the reader simply with a sweeping and lofty imitatio Christi injunction. He elaborates on several specifics of Christ's costly sacrifice for the church and then in 5:28-29 again admonishes husbands to love their wives as Christ loved the church and again elaborates on the application. Paul weaves a rich metaphor into this command by instructing husbands to love their wives as their own

bodies, tenderly nourishing and cherishing them just as Christ tenderly cares for and nourishes his body the church.

Paul then finishes this paragraph by noting the mysterious sacred "one flesh" intimacy of marriage which pictures Christ's union with the church. Thus, if Ephesians 5:24 is understood in its context, selfish mistreatment of wives by husbands is utterly precluded. In fact, this passage makes such selfish manipulations by dominating husbands a slanderous assault on Christ, for marriage is to be a most winsome picture to the world of Christ's love and care for his bride. (13)

Before Brian and I married, we agreed to not have sexual relations until marriage because of the biblical mandate to wait until then. Brian was adamant about this and I thought it was sweet of him to be so respectful of me and God's will. Boy was I fooled. It was just part of an image he wanted me to see.

After marriage, Brian required sex several times a day whether or not I wanted it. He would just show up and do what he wanted, ignoring my growing reluctance. Once I asked him why he thought he had a right to it so often, without my willing participation. His answer was matter-of-fact: "Because I am your husband and you have to submit whenever I want it." And that was that. It didn't matter I was exhausted from raising a baby, or unenthusiastic with the monotony of several quickies a day. He was my husband and my role was to submit regardless of my personal feelings.

It was also a type of "payment" to him for being able to stay home full time with our children. I felt guilty because I literally felt like a prostitute having to earn her room and board. I learned after I left Brian that this is sometimes called "passive prostitution."

Toward the end of our marriage, I told him "no" one day when he showed up and pushed me toward the bed. I was sick, and also worried about catching a disease from him. He grabbed me and pushed me toward the bed again. I pulled back and said "NO, not this time." Without saying a word, he grabbed me and forced me onto the bed and had his way.

I felt violated and completely broken at that moment. But it made little sense why I would feel that way since he was my husband right? Husbands can't rape their wives! Then why did I feel raped? Why did I feel violated, used and worthless? It feel like my spirit was dying. I slipped further into depression and hopelessness after that incident.

My feelings didn't subside even though I pretended everything was normal. In fact, right after that, he demanded I take pictures of him showing off his muscles because he was so impressed with himself. My life felt unbearably painful. Intertwined in this was his "spiritual speak." Everything felt confusing and conflicting.

After that while he was at work, I called a shelter and spoke with the Director. I shared with her some of what was happening and asked her if she thought I was going crazy. Her response changed my life. She said, "Robin, your husband raped you. Your feelings are normal and expected of someone who has been raped. Marriage gives no one the right to force themselves on their spouse. That isn't love. That is breaking the law."

I will never forget the overwhelming relief I felt at being listened to and validated. To know I wasn't crazy! My feelings were normal! To people who have not endured abuse in an intimate relationship, this sounds far-fetched. Only those who have experienced this know what I am talking about—the crazy making, the emotional roller coasters, the depth of fear and despair that never seems to end. The Director helped me to see the truth of what was happening—I was in an abusive relationship. It wasn't my imagination and our relationship wasn't going to get better.

This conversation was a crucial part of my journey to freedom.

That is why I encourage women who feel confused about their relationship to talk to advocates at a shelter. Just one conversation can shed light into a dark world.

Do you feel like you cannot talk to someone who may be an "unbeliever" or because a shelter or crisis center is a "secular" agency? As someone who worked in a crisis center and a shelter, I wish I could help you understand how special these people are. It's not a matter of you versus them. That's part of the isolation you are in. The people who volunteer and work at these places are some of the most caring people who will ever meet. Believe me, no one is there because of the money and status. They are there because they care deeply about this issue and want to help everyone they can. Go there for information and to talk to people who will listen non-judgmentally and support you.

Leslie Vernick, a licensed clinical social worker, insists on using correct terminology in her book *The Emotionally Destructive Relationship: Seeing It, Stopping It, Surviving It*:

> Submission is a discipline of the heart for all believers to practice, not just wives or women. All Christians are called to submit to authority (1 Peter 2:13), to one another (Ephesians 5:21), and to God (James 4:7). Please don't misunderstand what submission is and what it is not. In the Greek, the word submission (hupotasso) describes a voluntary action or attitude. Biblical submission cannot be forced. It is a position we take when we are motivated by our love for Christ and our desire to please and obey Him. Although God commands us to submit to Him, obey Him, and love Him, He never forces anyone to comply with His commands. He gives us a free choice, including freedom to choose badly (like Adam and Eve did).
>
> When a husband bullies his wife, his behavior does not

describe biblical headship, nor is her forced "submission" characteristic of biblical submission. The correct terms are coercion, manipulation, intimidation or rape and she is the victim. Let's make sure we use the right words. [Emphasis mine]

I am amazed in those instances when a man who believes so strongly in forcible submission is confronted with his own sin but is unwilling to submit himself to anyone else's authority for help and accountability, including his own pastor. He is not open to correction, challenge or change because he is always right. He manipulates the Scriptures to serve his purposes.

Jesus cautions those in positions of authority—parents, husbands, pastors and elders—not to misuse those God-ordained positions for self-centered purposes. These roles are given to us by God to humbly serve the individuals or groups that have been entrusted to our care, not to have our egos stroked or to get our own way. (Mark 10:42-45)

Sadly, some husbands have used their God-given position in their homes for selfish purposes, and often other Christians have unwittingly endorsed them. These husbands believe that they have license to do or demand anything they want, and that their wives are supposed to comply. This ought not to be. (14)

J. Lee Grady, an ordained minister and activist against abuse of women, explains in his article *The Dark Side of Wives Submitting to Husbands* that headship was never given as a license to control:

Marriage is not a hierarchy. Traditionalists assume that a Christian marriage is defined as a dominant husband who makes all family decisions while the wife graciously obeys without input. Yet Scripture actually portrays marriage as a loving partnership and refers to the wife as a "fellow heir of the grace of life." (1 Peter 3:7, NASB) And the apostle Paul taught that in the realm of sexuality, husbands and wives share equal authority over each other's bodies. (1 Corinthians 7:4) In other words, submission in this most intimate part of a marriage covenant is mutual, and this same mutuality is the key to any happy marriage; it fosters respect, communication, and an enduring bond.

Headship is not a license to control. Traditionalists also cite Ephesians 5:23 to remind wives that their husbands are their "heads" - and they believe this term requires some type of dictatorial control in marriage. Yet the Greek word used in this passage, *kephale*, does not have anything to do with heavy-handed authority, and it cannot be used to enforce male domination. Neither does it imply male superiority. The word can either mean "source" (as in the source of a river) or "one who leads into battle" (as a protector).

Neither original definition of this word gives room for abuse. Headship, in its essence, is not about who's the boss. Rather, it refers to the Genesis account of Eve being taken from Adam's side. The husband is the "source" of the wife because she originated from him, and she is intimately connected to him in a mystical union that is unlike any other human relationship.

Men who abuse their wives are out of fellowship with God. First Peter 3:7 is clear: *"You husbands in the same way, live with your wives in an understanding way, as with someone weaker, since she is a woman; and show her honor as a fellow heir of the grace of life, so your prayers will not be hindered."*

Wife abuse is no trivial sin. Any man who berates his wife,

treats her as inferior or engages in abusive behavior (including hitting, kicking, raping, cursing at or threatening punishment) will jeopardize his fellowship with the Lord. He will feel frustrated and convicted until he repents. (15)

Many abusive men hide under the disguise of Christianity and make a big deal of Ephesians 5 and similar passages. But the fact is these Scriptures condemn him. Abusers hate the truth revealed in these passages for they command him to love, serve and give himself up for his wife. That goes against his nature and character, which is to dominate her.

Mary Kassian, professor of Women's Studies at Southern Baptist Seminary, in her article *7 Misconceptions about Submission* says:

> A husband does not have the right to demand or extract submission from his wife. Submission is HER choice - her responsibility... it is NOT his right!! Not ever. She is to "submit herself" - deciding when and how to submit is her call. In a Christian marriage, the focus is never on rights, but on personal responsibility. It's his responsibility to be affectionate. It's her responsibility to be agreeable. The husband's responsibility is to sacrificially love as Christ loved the Church - not to make his wife submit...

> A Christian's first responsibility is to submit to the Lord and His standard of righteousness. A wife is not called to submit to sin, mistreatment or abuse. The Lord does not want "weak-willed" women - women who lack the discernment and strength to respond to the right things and in the right way. Godly women do not submit to sin. They carefully and intentionally weigh and discern how to submit to sinful human authority in light of their primary responsibility to submit to the ways of the Lord. No brain-dead doormats or spineless bowls of Jello here! Submission is neither

mindless nor formulaic nor simplistic. Submitting to the Lord sometimes involves drawing clear boundaries and enacting consequences when a husband sins. Submission is an attitude of the heart. A woman can have a submissive spirit even when saying "no" and refusing to go along with sin. (16)

Biblical headship does not remove his wife's right to choose. At the heart of domestic violence and abuse is the sinful use of a husband's power to gain control over his wife. How does that align with sacrificial servant hood? Just like Leslie Vernick stressed: use proper terminology! A husband demanding his own way and mistreating his wife is not biblical headship. It's selfishness, abuse of power, and condemned by God. It is often against the law too.

What causes a man to treat his wife in this way? Brenda Branson and Paula Silva explain it in their book *Violence Among Us: Ministries to Families in Crisis*:

> An attitude of superiority and a deep disrespect for women, combined with feelings of entitlement and desire for power and control, prevent the abusive man from feeling empathy or compassion toward his wife. He feels little or no remorse when he slaps her around because in his eyes she is always wrong; she is the one to blame. His goal is to discredit her, to silence her protests, and to divert attention from his bad behavior to her failures.
>
> Where do these attitudes originate? They typically result from 1) male role models in the home who disrespect or abuse women; 2) cultural attitudes toward women as servants or property; and 3) distortion of Scripture preached from pulpits of all denominations for generations, erroneously teaching that because God created Adam first, man must be superior to woman in every way–mentally, physically, and spiritually. The colloquial corruption of the King James Version's 'help meet'

in Genesis 2:18 into the so-called "helpmate" of tradition has been the source of many disrespectful attitudes toward women by Christian men. God does not give husbands the right to control or punish their wives.... Other Scripture passages about submission (such as Ephesians 5:21-32) have been distorted by abusive men against their wives. They ignore the foundation of submission... where husbands are instructed to love their wives as Christ loved the church.

What does that love and leadership look like? Christ's love did not exploit, exert power and control, intimidate, demean, verbally abuse, or use force or violence... He did not demand his rights. Instead, He humbled Himself as a servant and washed the disciples' feet. "Submission is not a right given to a husband to demand but a precious gift given willingly by a woman 'as unto the Lord' (Ephesians 5:22). When an abusive, power-hungry man demands submission as his right, it is no longer a loving gift but a stolen treasure gained by extortion and coercion. (17)

Do you wonder if submission will change your husband? Debi Pryde and Robert Needham in their book *A Biblical Perspective of What to do When you are Abused by Your Husband* address this:

An abuse victim may think 'If I submit to this mistreatment with a loving and good attitude, God will help me and intervene.' But submitting to unjustified, impermissible evil is never blessed or righteous, not the least because it means the abuser is reinforced in his habituated wickedness, as well as being passively encouraged to lose out on God's intended blessings promised to husbands who cherish their wives.

Being persecuted for righteousness' sake (i.e., our confession of Christ and our walk with Him) does not obligate us to passively receive or to submit to evil without resistance, but rather, the Scripture obligates us to overcome evil, actively. To be unwilling to expose a husband's abusive behavior is actually a profound lack of Christ-like love toward him and a selfish putting of one's own short-term safety ahead of his long-term spiritual good. (18)

God is good. He is a good Father who cherishes His daughters and does not want them to live sub-par inferior lives. You are meant for so much more than this! You are valuable and precious and have a God-given purpose in life. Don't let the enemy work through abusive men to keep you from fulfilling what God has called you to.

One day about two or three months before I left Brian, he was angry with me. I don't remember the exact issue now, but we were standing in the kitchen in an impasse. Brian stood still and stared at me speechless. I stared back, unsure of what was coming next.

Finally, he shook his head. "You know what Robin? That's one thing I could never figure out about you." He held up his thumb in front of my face then jammed it down on the counter top. "Every time I get you under my thumb, you crawl out. I can never get you to stay under my thumb." He shook his head at me as if I was a hopelessly naughty and willful child and walked off.

I thought, wow, did he say that out loud to me? Is that his goal? To break my spirit and gain total control over me? It was an eye-opening moment. This supposedly spiritual man hiding behind all this biblical gibberish and superiority was trying to break my spirit and gain control of me. He wanted me to submit and stay under his thumb. I felt stunned by the confession and committed to letting no one break my spirit.

Remember the definition Dr. Jeanne King gave for a true abuser: "The criteria for intimate partner violence consists of: possessiveness, controlling behavior, lack of empathy, externalization of blame, isolation of victimized partner, and the use of battering to create and maintain a relationship of unequal power."

That described Brian. I thought of him from then on as "The Thumb" to remind myself of his motive. His motive wasn't love. It was to have power and control. I never let him break me even though he came close to it many times. Somehow, I always got back up and kept fighting for my daughters and myself.

Pastor Jeff Crippen shares a helpful perspective on the perceived normalcy of abuse in his sermon *Bow Down, Tremble, and Pay Homage*:

> It is not normal in the Christian life to sin against someone, especially in an obvious, plain way (like abuse), and then be able to function without a violated conscience. To be able to go day after day without the thing weighing upon your conscience. To be able to sleep like a baby who has just thrown his oatmeal in his mother's face. This is NOT Christ. This is NOT the Spirit of Christ. You may have grown so accustomed to abuse that you think it is normal, and if the abuser professes to be a Christian, you may believe that this kind of thing is normal Christianity. You may be insistent that others accept you and the abuser 'just as you are'—because you have lived in the darkness so long that you do not recognize light (if you are a victim). And if you are the abuser, you believe that such evil is compatible with being a Christian. It is not.
>
> 1 John 4:20-21 ESV *"(20) If anyone says, "I love God," and hates his brother, he is a liar; for he who does not love his brother whom he has seen cannot love God whom he has not seen. (21) And this commandment we have from Him: whoever loves God must also love his brother."*

An abuser almost never does anything that he himself considers morally unacceptable. He may hide what he does because he thinks other people would disagree with it, but he feels justified inside... an abuser's core problem is that he has a distorted sense of right and wrong.

And therefore, we say it once more—the abusive person, the person characterized by a profound sense of entitlement to power and control, by profound justification for the evil he uses to obtain that power and control—is not a Christian despite an ability to offer "wonderful" prayer, to expound upon accurate biblical doctrine, to be even an apparent model of Christianity. Because he fails THE ultimate test of Christ—that he love Christ and that he love others. Satan appears as an "angel" of "light."

Matthew 23:13-15 ESV 13 *"But woe to you, scribes and Pharisees, hypocrites! For you shut the kingdom of heaven in people's faces. For you neither enter yourselves nor allow those who would enter to go in. 15 Woe to you, scribes and Pharisees, hypocrites! For you travel across sea and land to make a single proselyte, and when he becomes a proselyte, you make him twice as much a child of hell as yourselves."* (19)

As we have been learning, "submission" is not the problem. It is the way it is being interpreted that is causing strife in marriages. There is a huge difference between submissive love given freely from the heart, and coerced love by threats, abuse and ungodliness.

Men who are power-hungry and control oriented will misuse Scripture to get what they want. They take pieces of Scripture and twist it to serve their own selfish desires. God intends for us to read and interpret Scripture in context. We should embrace the whole Bible, not just bits and pieces. If abusers would read their favorite Bible verses in context, they would lose their justification for what they do. There is no getting around that believers in Christ are to be "imitators of God," walking in love. Any other doctrine is false.

> *"Therefore be imitators of God, as beloved children, and live in love, as Christ loved us and gave himself up for us, a fragrant offering and sacrifice to God."*
>
> Ephesians 5:1-2

Below, I summarize Pastor Mark Hallock's sermon *God's Design for Wives* (based on Ephesians 5:22-24). In it he shares seven things that biblical submission do NOT mean:

1. That the wife is in any way inferior to, or less than, her husband.

2. That the wife becomes a passive participant in the marriage.

3. Putting the husband in the place of Christ as if the husband is absolute authority... therefore, it does not mean putting the will of the husband before the will of Christ. This means that if the husband tells his wife to do something against the will of God, or contrary to the Bible, she can say "no."

4. Agreeing with everything her husband says and giving up independent thought.

5. That a wife gets her personal, spiritual strength from her husband. Rather, she gets her strength from God.

6. That a wife should give up her efforts to influence, guide, and help her husband be conformed to the image of Jesus. She can pray for him to be the leader God wants him to be.

7. Living in fearful intimidation of a husband who can strike

out in physical, emotional, or spiritual abuse at any point. (20)

I want to encourage you if you are struggling with feelings that there is no hope and you might as well give up. You may feel that life will never get better and that you don't deserve better. Or _____ (you fill in the blank). DON'T GIVE UP! Your children need you to stay strong and keep fighting. There are others who will someday need your encouragement and support to help them through their pain.

God has a plan for you. I hope that these excerpts from various pastors and leaders are helping you to see that God does not require you to endure a dangerous abusive relationship. In the next chapter, you will see that God offers concessions for getting out of these relationships. There is hope that all this pain you are experiencing will end with God's blessing!

In closing, I would like to share Dr. Steven Tracy's six principles regarding the parameters of female submission:

> 1. A wife must not submit to her husband when obedience to him would violate a biblical principle (not just a direct biblical statement).
>
> All but the most extreme fundamentalists agree that a wife should not obey her husband if it involves violating a direct command of Scripture. But many moral issues wives face today are not directly addressed in Scripture (internet pornography, in vitro fertilization, gambling, cosmetic surgery, abortion, sexual fetishes, etc.). If we accept the doctrine of the sufficiency of Scripture, then we must not restrict a woman's right to refuse to submit to her husband to those instances in which she can cite a direct biblical statement that contradicts her husband's command... Often a wife may not be able to point to a specific biblical text to justify her

objection to her husband's command but will only be able to appeal to her sense of the broad teachings of Scripture which she truly believes are applicable to the issue at hand.

2. A wife must not submit to her husband when obedience to him would compromise her relationship with Christ.

We have noted that Christ, not a husband, is a Christian wife's supreme Lord. She is Christ's bride first and foremost. The early Christian apostles were commanded by their religious authorities to quit teaching about Christ. Their response is instructive: "We must obey God rather than men" (Acts 5:29)... Modern Christian wives must recognize that their first allegiance is to Christ. Their husband is neither their priest nor their lord... Hence, a husband has no right to dictate his wife's relationship with Christ. In practical terms this means a wife should not obey her husband if he tells her not to go to church or to a Bible study, forbids her from going to a counselor, pastor or Christian adviser, or forbids her from spending time with a trusted friend.

3. A wife must not submit to her husband when obedience to him would violate her conscience.

Sometimes a husband will order his wife to do something that she cannot identify as patently unbiblical, and yet the behavior is internally objectionable to her. That is, it would violate her conscience. Again, based on the fact that Christ is her Lord, and based on Paul's teaching that we must always act in faith before Christ and not violate our conscience (Romans 14:22-23), a wife should not obey a husband if doing so will violate her conscience. This principle is particularly helpful in our culture when a husband requests his wife to participate in sexual practices that she finds objectionable.

4. A wife must not submit to her husband when obedience to him would compromise the care, nurture and protection of her children.

God calls adults to prioritize protecting and caring for the vulnerable, particularly children (Isaiah 1:17; Jeremiah 22:3). Care for the vulnerable, including children, is described as the purest form of religion (James 1:27). In Scripture, both fathers and mothers have a responsibility to care for their children physically and spiritually (Deuteronomy 6:4-7; Proverbs 31:10-31; Ephesians 2:7-8, 11-12). Thus, children are commanded to obey their fathers and their mothers (Proverbs 1:8; Ephesians 6:1)... We should particularly note that children innately develop their sense of God's character from their experience with their earthly father. So children whose fathers are abusive or harsh develop distorted views of their heavenly father. Thus, if a husband is harsh, verbally abusive, or uses excessive forms of punishment (including physical abuse), a wife has a moral obligation to protect the children regardless of her husband's requests or demands.

5. A wife must not submit to her husband when obedience to him would enable (facilitate) her husband's sin.

Not only are wives to avoid obeying a husband's command to sin, but they should also avoid following any commands that facilitate a husband's sin. The holiness of God requires that we not enable others to sin with greater ease.

6. A wife must not submit to physical, sexual or emotional abuse.

...It is thus important to recognize that enduring avoidable abuse, including at the hands of one's authorities, is not commended biblically. Scripture affirms the wisdom and propriety of fleeing an abuser, *"a prudent man sees danger and takes refuge, but the simple keep going and suffer for it."* (Proverbs 22:3) There are numerous biblical accounts of godly individuals who avoided physical abuse from their authorities (civic and religious) whenever possible... Not only is it entirely biblical for a wife to flee or otherwise refuse to submit to abuse of her and her children's physical and emotional well being, but not submitting to an abusive husband is also best for the husband. Wives are to do good to their husbands (Proverbs 31:12), and one of the best ways wives of abusive husbands can do this is by challenging the abusive behavior through fleeing, filing assault charges, contacting church authorities, or by otherwise stimulating real accountability and painful consequences for the abusive behavior. Refusing to submit to abuse and instead taking action to not allow it to continue is good for the husband because: (1) this is one of the best ways to break through the abusers' distorted thinking and stimulate repentance; (2) It decreases the temporal and eternal consequences that accrue the longer a husband abuses. In cases of unrepentant abuse, divorce may well be a tragic necessity. (21)

God knew some men would mistreat their wives and children. He knew many would do it in His name to justify their abuse and reinforce their assumed power and authority. So God did something loving for you. He laid out what His perfect plan was for marriage, and then He laid out concessions so that victims of abuse would have a way out. In the next chapter, we will look at these concessions. You probably know about two of them: abandonment and adultery. But there are more and they may apply to your situation.

Reflection: Self-Worth

Self-worth. It's how you feel about yourself as a person with value, regardless of your qualifications, appearance and achievements. It's associated with self-respect. Having low self-worth is damaging and may lead you to strive for an unrealistic perfection. Common associations with low self-worth are depression and guilt and you may try to prove your worth to others. A toxic relationship contributes to the loss of self-worth in the victim. Low self-worth will attract those with a predatory nature. Changing this is vital to protecting yourself and ending a pattern of dysfunctional relationships.

If you're lacking self-worth, you may feel withdrawn and unsure of yourself, uncertain of what you want and what you believe, worthless, unable to relax and enjoy life, and directionless.

If you know your self-worth, you will feel:

- Greater enjoyment of life in general
- Comfortable facing new challenges
- Excited about new opportunities
- Secure in your beliefs and opinions
- Respected by other people
- At peace with yourself and the world around you
- Sure of yourself and your ability to handle life's challenges
- Inner stability
- Pleasure from healthy relationships because you don't need them to compensate for a self-love deficit

EXERCISE:

Keep a daily list of about ten instances when you did something you feel good about. They may feel insignificant, but write them down anyway. Such as listening to someone, remaining calm with the kids, helping someone pick up their spilled groceries, smiling at the homeless person you walk by, going to the gym, or giving someone a hug.

Whatever it is, write it down and review it before you sleep. The point of writing it is that you re-experience these instances. You think about it. Your image of yourself will begin to transform into someone of value with something worthwhile to contribute to your family and society.

Why This Works:

- Re-experiencing positive events that happened ensures easy recall later when doubt creeps in
- Provides a timeline showing your growth and also pin-points the times when you got off track
- It magnifies the positive and minimizes the negative and the drama that comes with it
- Rejects inner critic thinking
- Proves to yourself that life is full of goodness and you can enjoy it
- Provides evidence of your self-worth

Tips to Take Control of Your Worth

Besides the exercise above, here are more ways to silence the inner critic and boost self-worth:

- Write a list of your past successes

    Think about the times in your life when you've been successful at something. Write a list of these times and remind yourself how you did it, how you felt and how great success was. Use this experience to nurture your self-belief and confidence.

- Silence the gremlin

    Pay attention to how many times you think or speak negatively about yourself. Exercise B will help you identify and silence the "gremlins" who try to pull you back.

- Don't compare yourself

    Instead of comparing yourself to others, notice the characteristics of people you admire. Pick up on their positive words and body language so you can add these to your own repertoire. Surround yourself with people who you would like to emulate, remembering that you are the best at being you!

- Accept compliments

    Being able to accept and feel good about compliments is crucial to cultivating self-worth. The best way to accept a compliment is to look at the person, smile and say 'thank-you.' Resist the temptation to critique it.

- Take care of yourself

    Take time out to nurture yourself. Exercise, cut down on alcohol, get enough sleep and feed your mind with positive messages. Remember you deserve to take care of yourself and be taken care of! Use the self-care checklist in Exercises F and G to make small daily adjustments and see you are worthy of being loved, respected and cared for.

"No one can make you feel inferior without your consent."

~ Eleanor Roosevelt

Foundation

"I thank you, God, for making me so mysteriously complex! Everything you do is marvelously breathtaking. It simply amazes me to think about it! How thoroughly you know me, Lord!"

Psalm 139:14 (TPT)

"I have never called you 'servants,' because a master doesn't confide in his servants, and servants don't always understand what the master is doing. But I call you my most intimate friends, for I reveal to you everything that I've heard from my Father. You didn't choose me, but I've chosen and commissioned you to go into the world to bear fruit. And your fruit will last, because whatever you ask of my Father, for my sake, He will give it to you!"

John 15:15-16 (TPT)

"We have become His poetry, a re-created people that will fulfill the destiny He has given each of us, for we are joined to Jesus, the Anointed One. Even before we were born, God planned in advance our destiny and the good works we would do to fulfill it!"

Ephesians 2:10 (TPT)

Chapter 12
Escaping the Ultimate Loneliness

"If you don't have a deep love relationship in your marriage, then you have a fake marriage. It may look good to others, but it doesn't look good to God... [Christians] teach that marriage is a set of vows and roles and behaviors. The Bible teaches that husbands and wives are one, and equal in God's eyes, but we set the husband above the wife. We teach that marriage is the lack of divorce... We have leeched out the true meaning of marriage and supplanted it with a formula that will produce a stable system with no life... God created marriage so that there would not be loneliness... so that humans could be fulfilled in an ultimate relationship. But our recipe for marriage creates the ultimate loneliness."

~ Don Francisco, Christian Musician

"**GOD HATES DIVORCE!**" "**Divorce is Sin!**" We hear that all the time don't we? By the time you finish this chapter, I hope you will view separation or divorce from a destructive relationship with a sense of God's love and compassion, rather than the condemnation and hopelessness that typically accompanies those statements.

Patriarchal religious leaders frequently counsel wives to provide to their husband the benefits of what would belong in a good marriage, but ignore the toxic environment he creates for her to perform those benefits in. They condemn any suggestion she complain or even consider a divorce from what amounts to an impossible and hellish life.

Though they may not intend to be cruel, their ignorance of the Bible and of domestic violence causes them to parrot what they have been taught. Since they are not on the receiving end of abuse, they can't step out of their narrow and privileged perspective. They do not understand what it is like to endure abuse. Therefore, it is easy for them to proclaim against the wife things like:

- Divorce is sin! YOU are breaking the marriage vow "'til death do us part."
- God said you cannot divorce for any reason!
- You and your husband are one for better or worse!
- Divorce is quitting! God never quits and you should be Christ-like.
- Divorce is your unwillingness to forgive and forget, so you must not even be a Christian!
- Divorce is self-righteous hypocrisy. You aren't perfect either!
- Only people who are selfish and prideful get a divorce!
- Divorce is open rebellion toward God, which is witchcraft!

- True love is unconditional. True love hangs in there no matter how bad it gets.
- Stay and Pray! God will reward your faithfulness in heaven.
- What God has joined, you must not divide! You will come under a curse if you do.
- God wanted you to marry him so he would come to salvation because of your humble faithfulness.

Ironically, it is those who are supposed to bring spiritual light that condemn perpetrators, victims and their children to spiritual darkness.

Abused wives struggle in their relationship with God, feeling He does not care and has distanced Himself from them. Some abandon their faith, not wanting to serve a God that apparently does not love them and condemns them and their children to suffer.

Abusers suffer also because it reinforces them in their delusion they are right and can act with impunity. They are helped along on their destructive path by the institution that is supposed to warn them of the consequences of their continued sin, and guide them toward right living and right standing with God.

Children often forsake anything having to do with God because of the religious hypocrisy they witnessed growing up.

The attitude behind most of these accusations and demands stem from an underlying bias that views control of women a right of men; an assumption that women are physically, mentally and spiritually inferior to men; and a distorted perception of God as Law Master and ally in the subjugation of women. We find this faulty belief system in many religions and Christianity is not immune. God says repeatedly in the Bible how much He hates injustice and oppression of anyone.

When the above statements are said to an abused wife, it is

nearly always said in a way that conveys SHE is the one who is selfish, unfaithful, self-centered and misaligned with God if she utters any unhappiness about her marriage. The husband's biblical responsibility is evaded, as if by reason of having male DNA he is exempt from abiding by the law of love.

The biggest danger in these traditional religious interpretations is that they demand simplistic answers to the reality of difficult and often dangerous relationships. They resist any moral imperative to act on behalf of the oppressed if the "oppressed" means they are female and have a wedding ring on. They ignore the majority of the Bible that demands mercy, protection and justice for victims. They protect patriarchal churches and leaders from controversy that may cause a loss in membership and dollars. Money, comfort and status, rather than moral excellence and truth, are still the driving force behind many religious leaders and organizations no matter how much they piously claim otherwise.

What is inarguable is that God hates divorce. However, the reasons God gives for it, and the reasons given by many religious leaders, are two different things. God hates divorce because it represents the failure of a man and woman to come together in the ultimate beautiful unity He designed for their pleasure and fulfillment.

Divorce represents pain and heartache. It represents a failure to love. Whether one or both spouses do not uphold the covenant, it does not matter. God doesn't care about gender. People are suffering in obvious and hidden ways, and that suffering breaks His heart, as it should ours. People are missing the joy and peace He wanted them to experience in their relationship.

When domestic violence and abuse is present, everyone in the family loses: they lose their trust, security, happiness, safety, respect and love. Some will make it through and live a good life despite the scars. Others are forever changed by it, enduring a lifelong cycle of personal relational dysfunction and heartache.

The Bible also clarifies that divorce was not a part of God's original plan for marriage. Common sense says sin destroyed much of God's original plan for the human race, so He made concessions out of His love, mercy, grace and plan of redemption. Women are not exempt from these concessions. Abused wives are not exempt!

It appears that the only New Testament concessions for divorce are adultery (Matthew 5:31-32) or abandonment by an unbeliever (1 Corinthians 7:15). As discussed in Chapter Ten, interpreting Scripture requires not just regarding specific statements about the sanctity of marriage, but also the context, God-inspired exceptions, and a cultural understanding.

Don Francisco explains the often-misused verse of Malachi 2:16, *"For I hate divorce, says the Lord, the God of Israel, and covering one's garment with violence, says the Lord of hosts. So take heed to yourselves and do not be faithless."*

> Of course, marriages are intended to be lifelong. But in this imperfect world divorce can sometimes be lifesaving... The widely used verse in Malachi where God seems to state that He "hates divorce" is mistranslated. What God hates is literally "the putting out" of a woman.
>
> Putting out is altogether different than divorce in Jewish culture. A man would permanently kick his wife out, denying her the Jewish divorce certificate. This woman would still be legally married, but with no home. Her dowry and children would be retained by the husband. She would have already surrendered her virginity to him. She would be ineligible to remarry, since technically, she was still legally bound to her husband. Further, her culture would label her as an adulteress since she did not have a valid divorce certificate.

And this lady couldn't just rent an apartment and get a job teaching kindergarten - there was no place for a put out woman in Jewish culture of that day except prostitution. Since the marriages were most often arranged, this whole horrible chain of events would have been completely out of her control.

The husband, however, was free to marry again and to do this as much as he liked. That is why Moses required a divorce certificate to be given... so that the marriage was legally, fairly, and religiously terminated and the woman would be free to remarry and go on with life... A Jewish divorce certificate is so valuable that often after a man puts out a woman, he will legally obtain the certificate and then sell it to the highest bidder...

All over the Bible we have ignorantly and clumsily translated "put out" as "divorce." This has caused many errant doctrines to be formed and made a terrible mess out of millions of people's lives. The toll in human suffering because of our ignorance is overwhelming. The Bible simply does not say that God hates divorce. It says that God hates the putting away.

In the New Testament, Jesus continues to address this cruel breach of human rights. Nearly all of the verses translated "divorce" in the Gospels actually say "put away." It is a completely different situation which we have no equivalent for. Knowing this makes a world of difference. For instance, many believe that Christian remarriage is adultery. But Jesus did not say that if a man marries a divorced woman, he would be committing adultery. He said that if a man married a "put out" woman, he would be committing adultery. This is because she was technically still married! In Israel, putting a woman out is a devastating, intentional ruination of a woman's life. God still hates it. (22)

This makes me think of Jesus coming to give us life: John 10:10 *"The thief comes only to steal and kill and destroy. I came that they may have life, and have it abundantly."* Jesus is talking about spiritual life and abundance. Look at the fruit of your pastor, husband and anyone else telling you in so many words to shut up and submit.

If Jesus is behind the message, it will move you into a life of peace and harmony. If "the thief" is behind it, it will steal your peace and joy, and kill your spirit, future, dreams and destiny. Primary to spiritual life is feeling safe, loved and respected in your own home. That is God's will for you, not control and domination.

Stephen Gola expounds on the Malachi passage in his book, *Divorce: God's Will?*:

> We have heard this Scripture: "the Lord God of Israel says that HE HATES DIVORCE" (Malachi 2:16). This is almost always quoted as if God hates all divorces in general. But that's just not true... there are TWO "kinds" of marriages and TWO "divorces" being mentioned in the Malachi 2:11-16 passage.
>
> The "divorces" were not official divorces; they didn't need to be. They were already previously married and "unofficially" married again. The Hebrew word shalach means "putting away" - a separation, as correctly translated in most Bibles. However, the King James and a number of newer versions have incorrectly translated shalach as to mean: divorce. It never meant divorce and it doesn't mean divorce. The word was most likely translated as "divorce" to fit what was taught in the church. Shalach is just a common word used throughout the Old Testament which means to: go, separate or to send. That's it!

So why did God angrily say that He "... hated putting away [a separation]?" "... Because you have not kept My ways [concerning marriage, divorce and remarriage] but have SHOWN PARTIALITY IN THE LAW" (Malachi 2:9). The Law specifically stated that when a man got a divorce from his wife that he was to write "... her a CERTIFICATE OF DIVORCE, put it in her hand, AND [shalach] send her out [put her away]..." (Deuteronomy 24:1)... Instead, men separated from their wives without ever giving them a Certificate of Divorce and then illegally married someone else. This is why the Lord said that they were still "their wife by covenant." The marriage covenant had never been dissolved by the Divorce Certificate.

The Lord's holy institution which He loves...the Lord has been witness between you and the wife of your youth ... [and] SHE [STILL] IS YOUR COMPANION AND YOUR WIFE BY COVENANT. For the Lord God of Israel says that He hates divorce [shalach], [separating without a Certificate of Divorce].... Because these men had remarried illegally — separated from their wives without giving them a Certificate of Divorce, they were in adultery as Jesus stated: "Furthermore it has been said, "Whoever PUTS AWAY [separates from {apoluo}] his wife, LET HIM GIVE HER A CERTIFICATE OF DIVORCE. But I say to you that whoever PUTS AWAY [separates and remarries without being divorced from] his wife for any reason except sexual immorality causes her to commit adultery: and whoever marries a woman who is PUT AWAY [separated without being divorced {apoluo}] commits adultery" (Matthew 5:31-32). (The Lord never forgot about the Malachi incident when He came to earth to redeem lost man).

Because these disobedient men still had "un-divorced" wives, the Lord did not command them to give their illegal wives a Certificate of Divorce, rather, they simply had to "separate, put them away, [shalach]." So did God hate divorce? No! Rather, God hated that the husbands were separating from their wives without giving them a certificate of divorce which would enable them to get remarried. This is what God hates! (23)

Pastor Jeff Crippen addresses the hypocrisy of those who get angry at the suggestion an abused woman divorce her husband in his article *Marriage, Divorce, and an Ox in a Well*. The truth in this article made such an impression on me that I am sharing it here in its entirety. I encourage anyone who struggles with these issues to read Pastor Jeff's books and articles on *A Cry for Justice*.

> Luke 14:1-6 "(1) One Sabbath, when He went to dine at the house of a ruler of the Pharisees, they were watching him carefully. (2) And behold, there was a man before Him who had dropsy. (3) And Jesus responded to the lawyers and Pharisees, saying, "Is it lawful to heal on the Sabbath, or not?" (4) But they remained silent. Then He took him and healed him and sent him away. (5) And He said to them, "Which of you, having a son or an ox that has fallen into a well on a Sabbath day, will not immediately pull him out?" (6) And they could not reply to these things."

One of the prevalent dangers in the church—especially in the conservative, Bible-believing church like the one I pastor—is that of falling prey to wooden, literalistic interpretation of Scripture that totally misses the heart of God and thus the real spirit of a particular passage. The error is the same as the Pharisaical handling of the Scriptures Jesus confronted here. The day of Sabbath rest was turned into "no work is to be done on the Sabbath," and that included even works that showed mercy to those in need. Nope, can't eat on the Sabbath if you have to make a sandwich—you can just go hungry. Nope, can't heal someone.

Jesus took these knuckleheads to their own hypocrisy. If their son or even their oxen fell into a pit or a well on the Sabbath, what was their common response? "He will just have to stay there and perish. He should have picked one of the other six days to fall in there. Look, everyone, at how holy I am. I am so pious that I am even willing to let my son suffer or die rather than violate this Sabbath day." Ooooh. Aaaaah. Yeah, oh man, what a holy guy. Not! God's love and mercy and care for human beings and even animals does not cease on the Sabbath! He still feeds them and cares for them and yes, even pulls them out of a well if they fall in. The Lord of the Sabbath effects works of mercy on the day of rest.

Now here's the deal. Abuse victims are in a pit. Yes, God's intent is that marriage be a blessing. A lifelong blessed covenant between a man and a woman. Love, honor, cherish—the whole thing. One flesh, self-sacrificing love. But sometimes it just isn't. Why? Because of sin. Because some husbands (and some wives) are just plain evil, cruel despots out to dominate and use and inflict pain. In other words, abuse victims have fallen into a pit.

So let me ask you this, Mr. or Mrs. preacher of "thou shalt never divorce for any reason, not even for abuse," what do you do when a dog is being cruelly treated by his master? A dog. Or a cat. Or a hamster. A horse. There the critter is, skin and bones out in the pasture. Starving. He knocks his water bucket over. Or the dog chews up a shoe (or commits some even more minor infraction like whining because he is hungry). You see the owner beating that animal and cursing it. Kicking it. Depriving it even more of food and water. Teasing and toying with it. What will you do?

Unless you are of the same ilk as that cruel master (and frankly, I believe that some of you people who mistreat abuse victims are indeed of the same ilk as the abuser), you will be reporting that cruelty to animals to the authorities and have that dog or horse or even a pet rodent rescued!! You will be calling for justice.

And so I ask you—no, no—JESUS CHRIST asks you, "which one of you, seeing a dog being beaten, will not rescue that dog from the 'covenant' of dog ownership?" The punch line almost need not even be stated, but here it is anyway:

"If you are ready to rescue a dog from cruelty and bondage, why do you refuse to rescue a human being from the same? Why do you forbid divorce, denying it to people who are wickedly treated and persecuted by a spouse who does not and never has kept the marriage covenant?" Many of you who preach this no-divorce for abuse line are very loud voices when it comes to the righteous opposition to abortion. And yet, when that baby whom you are so zealous to protect from violence now becomes an adult and marries a wicked man, you leave them in bondage even if their life is in danger.

God's mercy and kindness and His justice for the oppressed must never be sacrificed in our interpretation of His Word, else we join ranks with the Pharisees. Now go and learn what God really requires. (24)

Religious leaders have a choice. They can interpret Scripture with a heart that loves and cares about men and women equally. Or they can interpret Scripture to subjugate women. The Bible lists prominent and revered women leaders. Women held leadership roles in the early church. Nowhere in the Bible does God imply inferiority based on gender. It wasn't until the fourth century that men distorted Scripture against the equality of women and toward male superiority. This is a man-made religious addendum, not an actual biblical truth. Sadly, this has justified a pervasive abuse of women within the institution that claims to represent God's eternal truths. I can't imagine God is pleased to be represented in such a vile way.

Reverend Marie Fortune tackles the often used yet misquoted Matthew 19:6 verse in her book *Keeping the Faith: Questions and Answers for the Abused Woman*:

> "What therefore God has joined together, let no man put asunder." (Matthew 19:6) Any man who brings violence and abuse into his family life is putting asunder the marriage covenant that God has blessed. The violence is what breaks up the marriage, and the one responsible for that violence is the one responsible for the breakup. The actual divorce is in fact only the public acknowledgment of the private truth that a marriage covenant has been long since destroyed by abuse.

> "And this again you do. You cover the Lord's altar with tears, with weeping and groaning because (God) no longer regards the offering or accepts it with favor at your hand. You ask, "Why does (God) not?" Because the Lord was witness to the covenant between you and the wife of your youth, to whom you have been faithless, though she is your companion and your wife by covenant. Has not the one God made and sustained for us the spirit of life: And what does (God) desire? Godly offspring. So take heed to yourselves and let none be faithless to the wife of his youth. *"For I hate divorce."* says the Lord the God of Israel, *"and covering one's garment with violence"* says the Lord

of hosts. *"So take heed to yourselves and do not be faithless."* (Malachi 2:13-16)

We have always taught within the Christian tradition that the marriage covenant is broken by sexual unfaithfulness in marriage. The main reason that adultery is a problem is that it results in broken trust between husband and wife. But we should also realize that there are other kinds of unfaithfulness. Bringing violence into one's marriage is also unfaithfulness. Once violence has entered a relationship, trust is destroyed. If you can't trust your husband not to hit you, what can you trust? When God says in this passage that God hates divorce, God is acknowledging the pain that we all feel when a situation reaches the point where a divorce is necessary, when the brokenness is so great that it cannot be repaired. God does not say, "Thou shalt not divorce." But God grieves that unfaithfulness of any kind to the marriage covenant results in a divorce. (25)

I used to think a lot on the Matthew 19:6 verse of not dividing what God has joined. I felt that God had tried to warn me against marrying Brian, but I ignored it. I grew up believing if you were married, God was the one who put the relationship together, thus the sin of divorce. But my experience with Brian didn't agree with that belief any longer. I knew I jumped into my marriage with Brian out of my personal fears, desires and impulsiveness. I figured once I was in it, God would bless it because He had to right? Ultimately, He brought us together right? WRONG. To assume that is to avoid personal responsibility and the fact that God gives people a free will. So, what if God doesn't join every marriage together?

Stephen Gola addresses the question of unsanctified marriages:

We tend to think that EVERY marriage is blessed and seen as holy by God because of what we've been taught, but not every marriage is! God does not call holy that which is unholy. God desires us to be like Himself, to be able to "...distinguish between holy and unholy, and between unclean and clean" (Leviticus 10:10). If we do not have this discernment, we can make or continue in a fatal marriage. JUST BECAUSE WE ARE MARRIED BY THE LAW, IT DOESN'T MEAN THAT THE LAWGIVER HIMSELF HAS MARRIED US.

Many people stay trapped for years in marriages that God will not bless. Many are abused slaves to their spouse. They cry out, "Why doesn't God bless our marriage?" Blessings are given to the person who will call upon Him, love Him, and put Him first. God does bless us as much as He can, but many times it falls far short of what we really need because we block God.

Some unsanctified marriages... may have [husbands raping their wives, abuse, child sexual abuse, etc.] Some marriages have deteriorated over time, while others may have been bad from the start. Some unsanctified marriages may not have any outward manifestations of uncleanness at first. Some of the more common things that cause a marriage partner to be unclean are alcoholism, drugs, lustful sex, or a party spirit. The Bible has much to say about being a part of these things. Examples in the Bible are found in Ephesians 5:3-12, 1 Corinthians 6:9-11, and 1 Corinthians 5:1-13.

People live and die without ever experiencing the blessings that God pronounces on a sanctified marriage. They feel trapped and so continue in abusive situations because of what they have been taught (or not taught). For example, you may have been taught that once you've been married, you can never get a divorce because "God hates divorce", no matter how wrong, abusive, or unholy the marriage is.

The truth is, God is more for the divorce than He is for the marriage. But He IS able to change a heart to stop the unclean and unrighteous acts if that person will call out and yield their life totally to Him. (26)

Now we will look at eight things that break a marital covenant:

Abandonment

1 Corinthians 7:15 lists abandonment (desertion) as grounds for divorce. Abandonment violates the covenant by abdicating pledged responsibilities inherent in most marriage vows.

Your husband may leave your home without lawful cause and refuse to return. As a matter of delinquency, he may stop providing for your care, protection or support. For example, if you have health problems or minor children. Abandonment is the intentional non-support of the other spouse in destitute or necessitous circumstances and is grounds for divorce.

There is also the flip side called constructive abandonment. In this way he may make your life so unbearable in your home you have no other option but to leave. This might take the form of physical abuse or other acts that impair your health and make life intolerable. Or perhaps he changes the locks and prevents you from entering your home.

If he commits a crime, is convicted and sent to prison for a lengthy time—this may fall under the category of abandonment. He has knowingly placed himself in a position where it is possible he can no longer fulfill his pledged marital responsibilities. However it occurs, he has abandoned you. God permits you to seek a divorce in this case.

Pastor Jeff Crippen expounds on the concession of abandonment:

"But if anyone does not provide for his relatives, and especially

for members of his household, he has denied the faith and is worse than an unbeliever." (1 Timothy 5:8)

Now, Paul says that anyone who does not provide for his relatives, especially for his own family, has done two things: (1) He has denied the gospel. In other words, he is a practical apostate, and (2) He has revealed that he is an unbeliever of the worst kind. Worst, because many people who don't even claim to be Christians nevertheless care for their own families...

A true Christian is a new creation. He is indwelt by the Spirit of Jesus and taught by that Spirit. He is led by the Spirit and by the Spirit he puts to death the deeds of the flesh. Once a hater of God, he now loves God and loves God's Law. He does not need to be forced to love others, including his wife and children, and stop abusing them. If these things are not true of a person, then he is not a Christian at all...

Because this single verse says everything. A man who does not provide for members of his own household has denied the faith (no matter how much God-talk he spews) and is the worst kind of unbeliever...

We all know that all too frequently pressure is put upon abuse victims not to divorce their abuser. That is putting it mildly. They are frequently "forbidden" to divorce their abuser is more accurate. And one of the reasons given for this prohibition is that her husband "is a Christian" and she can only divorce (the claim goes) a spouse who is a non-believer and who doesn't agree to live together with her (1 Corinthians 7 normally cited and misused here).

But check it out. Paul says that the abuser is WORSE than an unbeliever! He isn't just an unbeliever who is ignorant of the gospel. Oh no. He is a person who KNOWS about Christ, who has professed Christ, who has "tasted" (Hebrews 6) Christ. And yet, he spits in our Lord's face and tramples on our Lord's blood by his wicked treatment of his own household. So of course an abuse victim has the right before God to divorce such a person. (27)

Adultery

Matthew 5:32 is cited as the other concession for divorce. Dr. Chris Trotter, an author and senior lecturer in social work at Monash University, and Michael Clanchy, a writer and counselor, explain why adultery (infidelity) can be as abusive as being hit:

> Why is infidelity abusive? Why is it sometimes a form of psychological and emotional violence? Because infidelity can be as devastating as a violent attack. It results in humiliation, hurt and loss for the injured partner. The betrayal is usually perceived as a direct attack on the faithful partner's worth as a person and as a partner.
>
> A research project involving in-depth interviews with a number of women and men who have experienced infidelity has been conducted at Monash University. The stories reveal numerous parallels between certain cases of infidelity and cases of psychological and physical abuse. The research found that common characteristics of abuse and infidelity include:
>
> - The Recurring Cycle. As with domestic violence, infidelity can become an ongoing feature of some relationships.
>
> - Similar Phases. Ongoing infidelity sometimes follows a path similar to the well-documented domestic abuse cycle. A typical cycle might include a tension build-up phase, the infliction of pain, a brief period of remorse

and guilt and then the reconciliation phase, followed by a return to tension build-up.

- Apparent Indifference of the Betraying Partner. Apart from brief periods of guilt and remorse after critical incidents of abuse or infidelity, the betrayers/abusers tend to be insensitive to the pain and distress they inflict on their partners. They often continue their infidelity or abuse without accepting responsibility for the anguish they cause.

- Similarity of the Responses of the Injured Parties. Those who stay for significant periods of time with partners who are unfaithful, often display the same psychological and social symptoms exhibited by victims of systematic abuse.

Some of these symptoms include deep personal suffering; low self-esteem and a sense of worthlessness; a sense of helplessness and a lack of control over their lives; a dependency on the betraying partner and a need for their approval; and a distorted sense of reality in which they can begin to believe that their partner's infidelity is their own fault.

Behavior patterns established by partners in abuse and infidelity situations can be difficult to change. Like domestic violence, unfaithful behavior does not often cease of its own accord, but calls for definitive action on the part of either the perpetrator, the affected party or both... Unfaithful behavior is heavily associated with lies, deception and denial. (28)

As pointed out by the research project at Monash University, adultery is devastating to victims in numerous ways. Under Moses' law, the penalty for adultery was death, a serious consequence! (Leviticus 20:10)

I love Jesus' response though, when He was challenged by the church leaders infuriated with a woman (not the man) caught in the act of adultery. His response was full of grace and wisdom: *"When they kept on questioning Him, He straightened up and said to them, 'Let anyone among you who is without sin be the first to throw a stone at her.'"* (John 8:7)

No one could claim to be without sin except Jesus. After the woman's accusers left, Jesus kindly admonished her to accept His forgiveness and continue her life with character and integrity. God still hates adultery, but through Christ's sacrifice and atonement on the cross, men and women guilty of adultery can repent and receive grace and complete forgiveness.

How the innocent spouse responds to the revelation of adultery is his/her choice. Some forgive a repentant spouse and move into a fulfilling and happy marriage. For others, trust is forever broken and repair of the relationship is impossible.

Not all adultery is abuse. It may be a symptom of a poor relationship that can be repaired. However, it may be just one more dynamic in an already abusive relationship.

Pastor Jeff Crippen shows how abuse and adultery is in fact desertion, and a concession for divorce:

> The victim of abuse, normally the wife but sometimes the husband, has a right before God to leave Egypt, to divorce the abuser. And I believe that anyone who comes to a true and proper understanding of the nature and tactics and evil of genuine abuse, will come to the same conclusion… I base my conclusion on 1 Corinthians 7:10-16 ESV:

> *"10 To the married I give this charge (not I, but the Lord): the wife should not separate from her husband 11 (but if she does, she should remain unmarried or else be reconciled to her husband),*

and the husband should not divorce his wife. 12 To the rest I say (I, not the Lord) that if any brother has a wife who is an unbeliever, and she consents to live with him, he should not divorce her. 13 If any woman has a husband who is an unbeliever, and he consents to live with her, she should not divorce him. 14 For the unbelieving husband is made holy because of his wife, and the unbelieving wife is made holy because of her husband. Otherwise your children would be unclean, but as it is, they are holy. 15 But if the unbelieving partner separates, let it be so. In such cases the brother or sister is not enslaved. God has called you to peace. 16 For how do you know, wife, whether you will save your husband? Or how do you know, husband, whether you will save your wife?"

Now, have you ever given real thought to just what it means to consent to live with a husband or wife? Or what it means (v 15) to separate from a husband or wife? Far too many Christians, I believe, conclude and assume that this simply means—to not file formal, legal divorce proceedings and to not physically throw the victim out of the house. I think that is the kind of application, or rather MIS-application that the Pharisees were characterized by.

Consenting to live with my wife, not separating from my wife, means rather that I keep my wedding vows made before God and witnesses to love, honor, cherish my wife. To live out a one-flesh relationship with her. To love her as Christ loved the Church and gave Himself for her. To refuse to do so, to have ill-will (malevolence) toward her, to see her as an object and a servant for my glory, is NOT living with her.

Abuse is, therefore, desertion. It is grounds for divorce. (29)

Adultery is often thought to just be illicit sex. However, the Jewish Talmud and Midrash also warn against "adultery" in reference to inappropriate thoughts and heart desire. It may have nothing to do with physical sex. Today, we refer to this as an emotional affair. Studies prove that emotional adultery, just as emotional abuse, is more hurtful than the physical act of sex or abuse.

Jesus, in His Sermon on the Mount, refers to emotional adultery when He says, *"But I say to you that everyone who looks at a woman with lust has already committed adultery with her in his heart."* (Matthew 5:28) Thus, Jesus indicates the heart has already engaged in adultery. Nothing there about it being strictly sexual!

Emotional affairs result in feelings of being lied to, deceived and betrayed, feelings similar to your spouse having an illicit affair. The key to determining whether emotional or physical behavior can be classified as an affair is if it is cloaked in SECRECY. Because a person's limited time, energy and affection are saved now for someone other than their spouse, it is easy for emotional abuse to be used against the innocent spouse as a way to help ease the guilt of what is going on secretly. No good thing can ever come of it and the damage cannot always be repaired. Victims of spousal affairs often say the worst part of the affair was not the act itself, but the deception.

Like any sin, emotional affairs don't stay just emotional. They start with a friendship commonly developed at work, church or through social media. Without safeguards in place and a healthy marriage, the friendship begins to meet the need for attention, affection and approval. If allowed to continue, it will eventually escalate into a full-blown sexual affair. Sex is just a natural procession of what is already active adultery, unfaithfulness and infidelity.

Besides adultery and abandonment, there are other heart issues that your husband may have that contribute to the breach of covenant in your marriage. Where adultery or abandonment are, there is some version of these next six apertures from marital unity.

Lust

Lust refers to "earnest desire." Again, it is a matter of the heart as Jesus pointed out. For example, if your husband longs for the non-sexual companionship or comfort of another woman, it may still be regarded as adultery.

Your husband promised when he married you to be faithful to YOU. You expected his heart's desire would remain for you. When his heart strays and his thoughts are with someone else, he is committing adultery. He may never touch her, and she may be unaware of his desire for her. But God knows. You probably suspect it, too.

Those who "earnestly desire" (the actual meaning of the Greek word we often translate as lust) another woman (for whatever reason), who have "set their heart upon" one other than their covenant spouse, are guilty of an inner breach of their covenant vows. (Matthew 5:27-28)

This includes pornography. I considered my husband's viewing of porn to be adulterous. His lust for alcohol and drugs was a losing battle too. Those always came first before the family. In both examples, my husband's thoughts and desires were for something or someone other than me. At first I tried to compete with both the porn and the alcohol/drugs, but soon realized that I could not. They would always come before me and be accompanied by lies, deception, risk of disease, risk of death and violence. His desire was bound to them, not me. He thought he could have a divided heart and it should not bother me. Realizing I was not a treasured part of his life was a crushing and devastating breach of covenant.

Idolatry

Greek scholar W. E. Vine informs us that the Greek word *moicheia* has a broader sense than the sexual. Vine points out that the concept of adultery is "breach of relationship." This covers any action and attitude that contributes to that breach of covenant. For example, he wrote,

> ... in Israel the breach of their relationship with God through their idolatry, was described as "adultery" or "harlotry"... so believers who cultivate friendship with the world, thus breaking their spiritual union with Christ, are spiritual "adulteresses" having been spiritually united to Him as wife to husband... It is used adjectively to describe the Jewish people in transferring their affections from God. (30)

Consider too, that idolatry and mental adultery combine in viewing pornography. A centerfold is a two-dimensional, lithographic "image" before which the lecherous worshiper bows in devotion.

Matthew 12:39, 16:4, and Mark 8:38, speak of a *"wicked and adulterous generation."* They were condemned for their lack of faith, disobedience and a sense of shame for the Lord and His teachings. This may have had nothing to do with sex. When we turn from God to the world, we break covenant with Him, and it characterizes us as a "wicked and adulterous generation."

Adultery is unfaithfulness in any form. The Bible links the concept of "adultery" with faithlessness to a covenant relationship with God. This may be brought about by many things, chief of which seemed to be idolatry.

In summary, the "essence of adultery" is unfaithfulness in a covenant relationship, which manifests itself in any number of ways. The outcome is the breakdown of the relationship, the violation of a covenant.

Physical and Sexual Abuse

Physical and sexual abuse of children or yourself constitute a complete and total breach of one's marital obligations and do not require you to stay bound to your spouse. It is based on the tragedy that many men violate God's design for marriage in the darkest, most destructive terms.

Paul describes marriage in terms of God's highest design. Husbands are to love their wives as Christ loved the church and gave Himself up for her. Ephesians 5:25-33 must be studied and taken seriously as to what the love of a husband looks like in a marriage. Love, in this passage, can be defined as a husband acting selflessly to meet the legitimate needs of his wife.

There is no way our loving Father condemns you for leaving physical and/or sexual abuse and getting a divorce. You need to protect children in particular if they are suffering sexual abuse, or are at risk. Get out and do it with God's full blessing and help. God does NOT require you to stay in that destructive, violent situation. The entire Bible condemns this abuse because it goes against God's nature and character. Reread the first section on abandonment. If physical and sexual abuse is taking place, there is no question that your husband has already abandoned you and the children. He has already broken the covenant. You are released.

Fraud

You married your husband believing there had been full disclosure. You find out later that he withheld information that would have adversely affected your decision to marry him. A "suppression of truth" becomes a "misrepresentation" which often has legal consequences. His intention must be to gain an advantage over you by withholding information. This is a faulty contract to begin with and God will not hold you to it.

While Brian's testimony included a general confession of a criminal life lived before Christ, he left out some significant information I would never have accepted for marriage, even with such an impressive testimony. He knew this and withheld it from me. This is fraud.

Fear for Your Life

You may have experienced an attempt on your life, or what you may consider a credible threatening of your life. For example, I became alarmed as, toward the end of our relationship, Brian repeatedly talked about how in prison he had learned how to kill someone and get away with it. He enjoyed describing the various methods. Since he knew I was unhappy with our marriage, I felt he was giving me a cloaked warning of what would happen if I tried to leave him. I lived in constant fear of dying from an "accident" or by "natural means" by his hands.

Dr. Robi Ludwig, author of *Till Death Do Us Part: Love, Marriage and the Mind of the Killer Spouse*, lists some traits of a potential spouse killer:

- Intense controlling behavior
- Explosive feelings of rage
- Difficulty forming intimate relationships
- Poor impulse control
- Inability to understand your feelings
- Absence of emotions like remorse and sympathy
- Searches out easy pleasure (i.e. a thrill seeker)
- Intense feelings of victimization and rejection
- Devalues human life
- Pathologically idealizes partner (31)

The National Center on Domestic and Sexual Violence has a revealing report on *Predictors of Domestic Violence Homicide*. It says:

> The strongest contextual risk factor for intimate partner homicide is an abuser's lack of employment" increasing the risk fourfold. The less education an abuser has increases

his violence as well. Other factors listed as predictive of femicide are: access to firearms, use of illicit drugs, living with the abuser before marriage, separating, having a child who is not the abuser's biological child, threats with a weapon, and threats to kill. (Note: other experts say threats to kill can be made subtly or directly—both are significant predictors of violence.) They also say an abuser's previous arrest of domestic violence *decreases* the risk for femicide. Arrest can be protective against domestic violence escalating to lethality. (32)

Passive Neglect

Pastor Jeff Crippen addresses the issue of men who are not violent, but rather passive and neglectful of their wife and family:

> ... There are some [men] who simply are passive. They are the sluggard of Proverbs 6:9-11, "(9) *How long will you lie there, O sluggard? When will you arise from your sleep? (10) A little sleep, a little slumber, a little folding of the hands to rest, (11) and poverty will come upon you like a robber, and want like an armed man.*"
>
> Is this abuse? What is the wife of such a man to do? We hold that an abuse victim is biblically justified in divorcing the abuser who torments her as he seeks power and control over her. But, what about this kind of passive neglect?
>
> Well, once again I think it helps for us to remind ourselves that marriage is a covenant. Scripture says so (Proverbs 2:16-17; Ezekiel 16:8; Malachi 2:14). And covenants have terms. Stipulations. They are made in the presence of God and witnesses, asking God to bless us for keeping the vows and to curse us if we break them. Pretty serious stuff...

The sluggard, in his passivity, is actively violating those sacred vows. Over time, as he persists in unrepentant sluggardly, not loving his wife who is his own flesh, he destroys the covenant. Is this abuse? Well, call it what you will, it certainly is unfaithfulness to the vow-terms of the covenant, and for that reason I maintain it is indeed grounds for divorce. The wife is not required to divorce him, but I believe a case could be made that she should separate from him and that her church should assist her in doing so. Why? Well, listen to this—

Thessalonians 3:10-15, *"(10) For even when we were with you, we would give you this command: If anyone is not willing to work, let him not eat. (11) For we hear that some among you walk in idleness, not busy at work, but busybodies. (12) Now such persons we command and encourage in the Lord Jesus Christ to do their work quietly and to earn their own living. (13) As for you, brothers, do not grow weary in doing good. (14) If anyone does not obey what we say in this letter, take note of that person, and have nothing to do with him, that he may be ashamed. (15) Do not regard him as an enemy, but warn him as a brother."*

We are not proposing here some kind of checklist procedure that is to be applied in every case like this, but surely we can see here that the Lord tells us how to deal with a man who passively abuses his family by not working, by not providing for them. (Incidentally, by "provide for them," we simply mean that he do so to the best of his ability). The church is to take this thing very seriously. Such a man, who professes to be a Christian, is living in a worse manner than an unbeliever! It is a shame to the name of Christ. We are to take note of him and have nothing to do with him. We are to warn him and pray that this process so shame him that he will repent. (33)

As I hope you can see, divorce is a biblical concession in our imperfect world for unfaithfulness in marriage. God knew in some marriages sin would create unbearable circumstances and there would need to be a way of escape for victims. The covenant is breached by the person choosing not to fulfill his or her part of the covenant. Divorce is a public and legal recognition of that breach. Blaming the victim for someone else's sin is wrong.

Idolizing the institution of marriage above the lives bound up in it is just that, idolatry and misplaced zeal. In God's love and compassion, He has provided a way of escape from terminally ill and destructive marriages. There is forgiveness, hope and a future free from spiritual condemnation.

Don Francisco offers a good closing of common sense and reality in his article *Marriage and Divorce Myth 2 - Is Divorce a Sin?*:

> It is impossible for all divorces to be automatically sinful because God has been through divorce. That's right, check it out in Jeremiah 3:8 *"Lo I had put her out and given her a certificate of divorce"*...He is speaking of Israel.
>
> Whether you consider this a literal divorce or not, if ALL divorces were a sin, you can bet those words would never have escaped Him... Both marriage and divorce can be sinful depending on the circumstances. In an absolutely perfect world, the union between a man and a woman would be perfectly initiated by God and there would not be any destructive forces tearing at the bond. Marriages would never break down.
>
> But this isn't a perfect world and some marriages become so emotionally, spiritually, and/or physically destructive that divorce can be life saving. That is why it is dangerous to slap a grid of legalism onto yourself or others.

The Bible does not forbid divorce, but God calls us to examine our hearts and to follow His specific leading. God wants us to live abundantly in His blessings. He will not entrap us, or force us to stay in our own traps to uphold an institution. The institutions of our loving God are never more important than the people within them...

Galatians states that we are no longer under law, but under grace. It is monumentally unhealthy to contend for a marriage on the basis that it is the legalistic and religiously correct thing to do... (34)

Perhaps you see you fall within the biblical guidelines for leaving your spouse. You are not just bored with your marriage and wanting to try something new. You are in a bad situation, there has been a serious breach of the marriage covenant, and you can see that God has made concessions for you to get out with no condemnation from Him.

So let's look now at options you may think about, such as separation, staying with him, counseling or divorce. We will examine how to settle the issue in a way that helps you experience God's peace and assurance with your choice.

Reflection: Transition

Transition. This is the time to make room for new happiness in your life. If you hold on to the pain and hurt, how can you be open to anything new? There is only so much space in your life. If your cup is full, empty it out little by little so there is room to fill it with new good things. Even though it is hard, later you will recognize how releasing the old was the catalyst for new beginnings and opportunities coming into your life.

As you heal and grow, memories will crop up and the temptation will be there to fall into a memory loop. You have a choice whether to go there. Instead of passively traveling down memory lane, acknowledge them and then bring yourself back into the present moment. Remind yourself that it's okay and none of it defines you or your future. What is going right for you now?

Questions to look forward:
- What future do you imagine for yourself?
- How will you bring your imagined future into reality?
- Who will hold you accountable?
- What is one step you can take today or tomorrow to move forward?

> *"You can't possibly embrace that new relationship, that new companion, that new career, that new friendship, or that new life you want, while you're still holding on to the baggage of the last one. Let go… and allow yourself to embrace what is waiting for you right at your feet."*
>
> ~ Steve Maraboli

As you make room for possibility, you will experience changes:
- A new positive you that feels great
- Increased confidence
- Discovering new things you enjoy
- Ability to handle new obstacles successfully
- Inspiring others
- Naturally attract what you need
- Empathy for others expands
- Knowing in your heart what is good for you

- New relationships come that bring joy

Tips for Finding Happiness

- Look within for your happiness
- Give thanks every day for the wonderful things in your life
- Get healthy
- Focus on the present
- Spend time with people who lift you up
- Enjoy hobbies and activities you are interested in
- Be curious and explore new things
- Do things to refresh, renew and soothe your soul
- Accept your history and the people who helped make you into the beautiful person you are today
- Have fun. Love yourself, love others and love this life
- Review your core beliefs/values and decide if they align with your goals. If not, create new ones
- Write 3 actions you will take this week to get yourself moving
- Be patient and gentle with yourself during this time of transition
- Volunteer or otherwise find some way to help others that you enjoy

> *"Some changes look negative on the surface but you will soon realize that space is being created in your life for something new to emerge."*
>
> ~ Eckhart Tolle

Foundation

*"I will instruct you and teach you in the way
you should go; I will counsel you [who are
willing to learn] with My eye upon you."*

Psalm 32:8 (AMP)

*"Trust in and rely confidently on the Lord with all
your heart, And do not rely on your own insight or
understanding. In all your ways know and acknowledge
and recognize Him, And He will make your paths straight
and smooth [removing obstacles that block your way]."*

Proverbs 3:5-6 (AMP)

*"For I know the plans and thoughts that I have for
you,' says the Lord, 'plans for peace and well-being and
not for disaster, to give you a future and a hope."*

Jeremiah 29:11 (AMP)

*"May the God of hope fill you with all joy and peace in
believing [through the experience of your faith] that by
the power of the Holy Spirit you will abound in hope
and overflow with confidence in His promises."*

Romans 15:13 (AMP)

Chapter 13

Options

BEFORE I MADE my final decision to flee from Brian, I explored other options. In this chapter, I want to talk about some spiritual issues I grappled with in association with these options. Maybe it can help bring clarity to your own situation. Figuring out what to do about an abusive relationship is complex, confusing and further complicated by religious beliefs. There are numerous dynamics involved, particularly if there are children. There is rarely one perfect solution, and each option has its own advantages and risks. People who don't understand abuse and the accompanying impoverishment think victims should "just leave." As we know, it's not that simple.

Staying

At first, I tried to just live with Brian's increasingly toxic behavior. I pacified him, catered to him, and pretended to him, myself, my kids, and other people that everything was great in our lives. That described this phase the most: agonizing pretense. Living a lie is hard work!

To create and maintain a pretension of something untrue, we must allow our authentic selves to die. We must become untrue to our own uniquely created and gifted person. This is painful because it goes against what God wants and what He created us to be. Worse, we aren't even able to reach out to others, either to receive or give help and support. Our world closes in and it's suffocating.

Everything good we care about must die as our abuser takes over our identity. That is the price paid for staying with an unrepentant abuser. For me, staying with Brian meant I compromised, forgave, submitted, gave in… I nearly gave up. He did none of those things for me and our relationship. It was me doing the giving and changing.

This is WRONG and why understanding the true biblical definition of submission is so important. An abuser's definition of "submission" is anything but biblical! All it does is feed sin (abuse), and sin is never satisfied! It always demands more until it has sucked away every ounce of life and individuality the victim has.

June Hunt, founder of the ministry *Hope For The Heart*, offers a six step strategy to counter verbal and emotional abuse if you want to stay in the relationship. Depending on the severity of abuse in your home, these suggestions may work. They did not work for me because Brian didn't see me as someone who had a right to independent thinking or acting. Any attempt at standing up for myself was met with stony angry silence at best. However, they might be helpful for you to try:

1. Clearly state what you are willing to accept and are not willing to accept from the abuser. Communicate your position in positive terms. Keep your statement short and succinct. Don't justify and don't apologize. Simply state

your boundaries. "I want our relationship to continue, but I'm not willing to listen to name calling.... I'm not willing to hear your accusations.... I'm not willing to endure any longer the onslaught of profanity."

2. Announce the consequence you will enforce if the abuser violates your boundary. Consequences are part of God's divine plan that what we sow, we will reap. Galatians 6:7 (NIV) states, "A man reaps what he sows." Repercussions should include disengaging or distancing yourself from the abuser. You can't change the abuser, but you can remove yourself from frequent exposure to unacceptable behavior. "I want to be with you, but if you call me any kind of name again, I will leave for a time.... If you persist in making that accusation, I will end our conversation.... If you choose to use profanity, I will choose to be with others where we can share positive, healthy conversations."

3. Enforce the consequence every single time the abuse occurs. Do not bluff! The abuser needs to know that you will follow through consistently. Plan on being tested multiple times. In your mind and heart, say no to manipulation, no to pressure, no to control. Eventually, there's a good chance your abuser will stop... but only after the behavior proves to be ineffective. James 5:12 (ESV) says, "... let your 'yes' be yes and your 'no' be no."

4. Absolutely do not negotiate. Since abusers do not use words fairly, negotiation will not work. Instead of "talking out" the problem, your abuser will seek to wear you out! Therefore, state that when the negative behavior stops, you look forward to a renewed relationship. "I am not willing to discuss this topic further.... I've stated clearly what I will not accept.... When you're ready to respect my requests, let me know. I look forward to being together at that time." Keep your words brief and to the point.

Proverbs 10:19 (NIV) warns that, "Sin is not ended by multiplying words, but the prudent hold their tongues."

5. Never "react" when your boundary is violated... only respond. Expect your boundary to be violated again and again! If you react, you will find yourself back under the abuser's control. Respond by detaching yourself from the abuser and enforcing your repercussions. Expect your abuser to use manipulative maneuvers. Don't cry. Don't beg. Don't explode. Expect your abuser to have emotional ups and downs. Expect your abuser to be angry with the boundary you have set. But don't seek to placate—it won't work. Take to heart Ecclesiastes 7:8-9 (NIV): *"The end of a matter is better than its beginning, and patience is better than pride. Do not be quickly provoked in your spirit, for anger resides in the lap of fools."*

6. Solicit the support of one or two wise, objective people to help you through this process. Include supporters as you analyze the problem, formulate your plan and enforce the repercussions. Trusted individuals—friends, mentors, counselors—can help you through this critical period. Discuss the situation with your supporters, including tactics used on you. Proverbs 19:20 (NIV) says, *"Listen to advice and accept discipline, and at the end you will be counted among the wise."* (35)

If you stay, what are the ramifications to your children?

Domestic abuse and violence doesn't only affect you. You may think, as I did, that if there is no physical violence then kids aren't affected. But they are. They are keen observers and they are learning about relationships from the example set before them. Growing up in a dysfunctional home sets them up to repeat the cycle of abuse in their own relationships because they think it is normal. Children's tender spirits are sensitive to the stressful unhappy atmosphere of the home.

According to Alison Cunningham & Linda Baker at the *Centre for Children and Families in the Justice System*, there are 10 effects on a child in an abusive home. The source for this is an excellent free PDF explaining the effects of abuse on mothers and their children and I would encourage you to read it in full: *Little Eyes, Little Ears. How Violence Against a Mother Shapes Children as They Grow.*

- Children are denied a good father and positive male role model.
- Abuse can harm the mother/child bond.
- Children can develop negative core beliefs about themselves.
- Children can become isolated from helpful sources of support.
- Unhealthy family roles can evolve in homes with domestic violence.
- Abuse destroys a child's view of the world as a safe and predictable place.
- Abuse co-occurs with other stresses and adversities with negative effects.
- A child's style of coping and survival may become problematic.
- Children may adopt some of the rationalizations for abuse.
- Children can believe that victimization is inevitable or normal. (36)

Cunningham and Baker also explain the effects of coercive control tactics on a mother though I will just list them briefly here:

- Woman believes she is an inadequate parent.
- Woman loses the respect of some or all children.
- Woman believes man's excuses for abuse and reinforces them with children.

- Woman changes her parenting style in response to abuser's parenting style.
- Woman's capacity to manage is thwarted or overwhelmed.
- Woman may use survival strategies with negative effects.
- Woman's bond to children is compromised.
- Woman gets trapped in competition for children's loyalties. (37)

Lindsey Holcomb and Justin Holcomb expound at length on the effects of domestic violence on children in their book *Is It My Fault: Hope and Healing for Those Suffering Domestic Violence*. In summary, they say:

> To begin with, studies suggest that between 10-15 million children are exposed to domestic violence every year. And for these children, abusive adults can cause tremendous long-term physical, emotional, and spiritual damage in their lives. This is true even if they [the abusers] physically abuse the mother (but the children are not physically hurt), though roughly half of men who physically abuse their wives also abuse their children. Bruce Perry, one of the top neurological trauma researchers in the world, has conclusively shown that when young children merely witness domestic violence, this trauma exposure creates long-term physiological changes, including significant structural alteration and damage to the brain.

Lindsey and Justin go on to describe the "aftermath of abuse" in children: higher suicide attempts, drug and alcohol abuse, running away, prostitution, committing sexual assault crimes, emotional and behavioral disturbances, feelings of powerlessness and humiliation, loss of innocence and feeling safe, anxiety and fear, self-blame, shame, responsibility, guilt and anger. They continue:

And here, among children, we see one of the most toxic effects of the cycle of abuse: Witnessing violence from one parent or caregiver to another is the strongest risk factor of transmitting violent behavior from one generation to the next. Boys who witness domestic violence are twice as likely to abuse their own partners and children when they become adults... girls who grow up in physically abusive homes are more likely to be physically and sexually victimized by their own intimate partners in adulthood... Children who've grown up in abusive households are 15 times more likely to be abused by other adults.

If you are reading this and are still on the fence about getting out of the relationship... studies point to destructive effects of abuse that are long-term. Even if your child has not personally suffered abuse yet, the consequences of even witnessing it in the home over the rest of their lives could be catastrophic. (38)

As if this isn't enough, another issue we as mothers must grapple with is, *What if I leave and he gets custody of the children? Then I won't be there to protect them. At least now, I am in the home and able to care for them.*

That is a valid concern and one that has no easy answer. However, just being aware that your children are being affected gives you power to counter the effects as best you can. Instead of just hoping for the best, you can protect and help them. In addition, Appendix G has applicable Bible verses you can pray over yourself and your children during this difficult time of life.

How are you affected? Staying with an abuser is spiritually risky. Has your husband's sin become malignant to your faith? Are you weakening spiritually and straying from your marriage vows? Are you looking at porn with him, drink and drug to please him or soothe your own pain? Are you finding yourself drawn to the comfort and attention of another man?

Your husband's sin is not a license for you to sin. This will only cause more problems, guilt and regret. Also, any questionable behavior you engage in now will be used against you down the road as 1. A personal unforgivable judgment against your character and 2. Your husband will use it against you legally. People ignorant about the dynamics of abuse will grab hold of any little straw and use it to build a monumental case against you, your character and your competence.

Since most abusers are charming, persuasive and unhampered by conscience, they will relish swaying everyone's opinion against mean selfish you, and for poor innocent him. Unfair? Yes it is. That is the reality. That doesn't mean you can't overcome it. It's just going to be a battle and the less you have to explain later on, the better.

Another reason you may have for staying is that you think God is punishing you for being a bad Christian or for past mistakes.

I hope by now that you see how much God loves you and does not punish you for the past. We all make bad choices and end up in bad situations at times. God is not punishing you for that. Making occasional mistakes is not remotely close to being habitually controlling and abusive. This book is about unrepentant and deliberate abuse as defined in Chapter 5.

Reverend Marie Fortune says in her book *Keeping the Faith: Guidance for Christian Women Facing Abuse*:

> There may be things in your past that you regret having done or that you are not particularly proud of. There may be sins of which you have not repented. You may not go to church regularly or do all the things that you think make a good Christian. But no matter what kinds of things you have done or neglected to do, you do not deserve to be abused, and

God does not send this abuse to you as punishment. If there are things that you carry that you want to repent of, then talk to God about those things in prayer. But do not excuse your husband's abusive behavior by deciding that it is God's will for you. The battering is not God's fault; it is the responsibility of your husband. He has chosen to treat you this way; it is not God's will for you. (39)

God does not want you ensnared in things that damage you spiritually, emotionally, mentally or physically. Your husband is not worth losing your peace, faith or integrity over. He is not worth your children growing up emotionally and spiritually bankrupt.

The consequences of staying in an atmosphere of sin and rebellion can have devastating effects on you and your children. There is a difference between staying out of guilt and fear, and staying with a plan in place and peace in your heart. Chapter 16 will deal with the paralyzing giant of fear so you can make decisions with peace and assurance.

You and your children are precious to God! That's why God has made separation and divorce a concession in grace on behalf of you, the innocent party, so you can leave the destructive environment and be safe. God not only offers divorce as a concession, but promises to walk with you through every phase of your relationship. He will not abandon you.

Separating

If you think you are trapped with no way out, but are not ready to pursue a divorce, consider an informal or legal separation. This can provide time and distance to cool off and decide if you feel the relationship is redeemable or not. Of course, your husband has to be okay with this. Brian wouldn't let me do this no matter how reasonable my arguments for it were. But perhaps it is an option in your case.

If your husband claims he will change, then separation can be a good time for you to do self-care, reflection and healing. A *Batterer's Intervention Program* for him and counseling for you, along with additional support from others can make a world of difference in reducing the confusion and imbalance you feel.

I recommend attending domestic violence support groups at your local women's shelter, crisis center or church. The knowledge you will gain from it, and the friendships you will make with others experiencing the same thing you are, will be life changing. It will also take time to see how committed he is to changing.

I asked Brian for a temporary separation but was denied. He wouldn't even comment on my requests. For him there was no issue that needed resolved, except for me to shut up and be happy with what I had. Occasionally he would tell me, "You will never find anyone as good to you as I am. You should be grateful you have it so good."

Nonetheless, I asked about three times, offered practical solutions to any obstacles, and promoted the positive things it could do for our relationship. At that time, I was still under the illusion that our problems could be fixed if I tried harder. I saw it as an "us" or "me" problem. I didn't yet see it as a "he is a batterer I cannot fix" problem. I also assumed he cared about our relationship and would want to do something to help it.

After he won me over into marriage, Brian did not show respect for me or interest in my needs or ideas. He didn't believe I would ever have the guts to leave since I was a full-time mother and dependent on him. He refused to acknowledge that there was any problem between us, and if there was no problem, then there was nothing to fix. He met my grief and heartache with stony silence and then perhaps a demeaning change of the subject as if I had said nothing. Or he would demand sex.

I finally realized that I had to make a choice. I either stayed, knowing the girls and I were in harm's way, or I had to get us out. I knew Brian would never let us walk away. I made a strategic plan of escape with some trusted people and followed through. After we left and he realized we were not returning, Brian waffled between phony remorse and venomous threats.

However, just a short time away from him helped me to think more clearly and see him for the controlling manipulative abuser he was. Trying to see it when I was with him was like looking at him through a dense fog. Distance from him brought clarity and perspective and allowed me to talk to other people without fear of reprisal. I never returned home, and he showed himself over the following year to not love or care about the girls or I.

The emotional and psychological hell of trying to detach from Brian and keep the girls safe was worse than when we had lived with him. But God... I could never have done it without Him upholding me every day. He brought us through and opened my eyes to see that what I had thought would just be a temporary separation from Brian needed to be permanent. The resulting hardship was worth it to have the lives of peace, freedom and joy we now enjoy.

Every situation will be different. Don't be afraid to do what you have to do to protect yourself and your children. It will be hard, but it will end eventually. The time after I left Brian was harder than the time I was with him. Leaving an abuser, even temporarily, is no cakewalk.

But you can do it and come out the other side so much better off. Things won't always go the way you want them to. That's why prayer, listening to your instincts, and receiving wise counsel and support from others is so important. We all need each other. This is a battle you aren't meant to figure out and fight alone.

Remember that the risk of lethality goes way up when you leave an abuser. It's the most dangerous time period, so I recommend surrounding yourself with a support system from your local women's shelter before you leave. Even if you think he won't do anything, leaving even for just a little while can trigger a nasty response you don't expect. He believes you and the children are his property. Protect yourself and be smart, but don't stay just because of the risk.

Appendix C has a risk assessment and Appendix D has a good safety plan.

Counseling or Mediation

Counseling should be individual, NOT couples counseling. In an abusive marriage, couples counseling is inappropriate and will make the abuse worse.

I also advise against turning to your pastor for counseling unless you know he has been trained in the dynamics of domestic abuse and violence. Otherwise, you will probably be sent back to your husband and your situation will worsen. Appropriate clergy involvement is explained in the next section.

Pastor Jeff Crippen advises those considering counseling or mediation:

> When we are dealing with an abusive person, the solution is not to just "sit down and talk, work things out, communicate and understand one another better." NO! Because as we have been learning, the abusive man or woman has no intent at all to work things out. He or she knows nothing of compromising, of empathizing, of kindness. He only knows

power and control and entitlement. Therefore, any such meeting with an abuser will only result in giving the abusive man another opportunity to abuse his victim.

This is a vital lesson to learn then in respect to dealing with an abusive person. Such a person... has only one purpose—to destroy, to discourage, to instill fear, to mock and rob his victim of any sense of self-worth and confidence... to control, to own, to exercise power, to be as God to his victims. Therefore, it is not wise to enter into mediation with an abuser. It is not wise to enter into couples' counseling with an abuser.

Communication problems are NOT the problem. The abusive person's mentality is the problem, and it is his problem alone... Like Nehemiah in his dealings with Sanballat [Nehemiah 6:1-13], the Christian is NOT bound to meet with an abusive person. We are NOT obligated to maintain an abusive relationship, thereby permitting the abuser to continue in his power and control and abuse...

Mediation, communication, reconciliation and peace-making requires goodwill from both parties. But as we have seen, the abuser has no goodwill—he is malevolent toward his victims. He will only use such sessions to exercise more of his abuse, to work more of his deceptions, and to make it appear to the foolish that he is the one who truly wants to set things right. (40)

Turning To the Church for Help

This is a topic I feel strongly about. I have, more often than not, witnessed the devastating effects of clergy discounting a victim's disclosure of abuse. When men of the cloth minimize us as abuse victims, it carries an extra load of pain because we trust them and their representation of God's values. Christian leaders are supposed to live by a higher standard, yet often they act in ways that are an affront to God.

That said, there are religious clergy, leaders and influencers who do "get it" about domestic violence and they are speaking out about it. There is an increase in domestic violence training in churches and a growing awareness that the church has long dropped the ball on this vital topic. I include links to many of these people in the resources section and encourage you to visit their websites for in-depth help.

I do not recommend turning to the church first, if at all, for help.

The feelings of shock, betrayal, disappointment and probable shunning hits victims hard, especially when they are at their weakest. They assume that the leadership at their church will understand their plight and have compassion and good counsel. They assume church is a safe place for them. Instead, leadership will usually blame the victim and justify the abuser. Even more so if the abuser has a valued position in the church. It's painful to experience on top of everything else going on.

If you are blessed to be part of a church that understands the truth about domestic violence and responds appropriately, then by all means utilize their support and be thankful for such a blessing! Let other victims know it is a safe church for them.

Reverend Marie Fortune expresses well the reality of religious betrayal:

> If you have not yet talked with your pastor or priest about the abuse you have experienced, there is probably a good reason. You probably intuitively sense that he or she will not be helpful to you. This may be because you have never heard

your clergy person mention anything about wife abuse. Or it may be because you have heard something mentioned that made it clear that your experience would not be understood or believed. Trust your feelings about this. Do not go to this person unless you feel safe and assured that your clergy person will listen, understand, and believe you. If you are simply unsure, take someone with you—preferably a shelter counselor or support group leader who can support you and help your pastor or priest learn about your situation. (41)

Carolyn Heggen, author of *Sexual Abuse in Christian Homes and Churches* says:

The church, past and present, has accepted and promoted a patriarchal agenda. In its teaching, practice, exegesis, and preaching, the church has perpetuated an ideology about men, women, and children in general - and about sexuality and abuse in particular - which has sustained the very foundation of the widespread problem of sexual violence... For every minister who says, "But no one ever comes to me with this problem!" there are dozens of victims, survivors, and perpetrators who desperately need the ministry of the church.

Whether through passive denial or active efforts to silence victims and survivors, the church contradicts its own mandate to justice... In fact, Scripture mandates the church to stand with those who are objects of harm and exploitation, to protect the little ones, to offer hospitality to the vulnerable, to set free those imprisoned by social convention. Jesus' ministry with women and children provides an unequivocal model of justice-making as the appropriate response to the injustices heaped on the oppressed. (42)

Pastor Jeff Crippen lays out a typical church response to abuse scenario in his book *A Cry for Justice: How the Evil of Domestic Abuse Hides in Your Church*. In my experience also, this is how it plays out. It doesn't vary much, and neither does the resulting devastation. Consider this scenario before you turn to your church. If you have already experienced this, then just knowing you are not alone may be of some comfort.

1. Victim reports abuse to her pastor.
2. Pastor does not believe her claims, or at least believes they are greatly exaggerated. After all, he "knows" her husband to be one of the finest Christian men he knows, a pillar of the church.
3. Pastor minimizes the severity of the abuse. His goal is often, frankly, damage control (to himself and to his church).
4. Pastor indirectly (or not so indirectly!) implies that the victim needs to do better in her role as wife and mother and as a Christian. He concludes that all such scenarios are a "50/50" blame sharing.
5. Pastor sends the victim home, back to the abuser, after praying with her and entrusting the problem to the Lord.
6. Pastor believes he has done his job.
7. Victim returns, reporting that nothing has changed. She has tried harder and prayed, but the abuse has continued.
8. Pastor decides to do some counseling. ...
9. As time passes, the victim becomes the guilty party in the eyes of the pastor and others. She is the one causing the commotion. She is pressured by the pastor and others in the church to stop rebelling, to submit to her husband, and stop causing division in the church.
10. After more time passes, the victim separates from or divorces the abuser. The church has refused to believe her, has

persistently covered up the abuse, has failed to obey the law and report the abuse to the police, and has refused to exercise church discipline against the abuser. Ironically, warnings of impending church discipline are often directed against the victim!

11. The final terrible injustice is that the victim is the one who must leave the church, while the abuser remains a member in good standing, having successfully duped the pastor and church into believing that his victim was the real problem. (43)

I see this scenario repeatedly played out in the lives of women I serve, not only for laywomen in the congregation but also for wives of abusive church leaders and pastors. It is also common that when the wife leaves the church and attends another, the abuser will follow her and turn the new church against her. He will do this repeatedly, making it impossible for her to attend any church in peace. The church believes her abuser's claims right away and frowns at her for causing problems and making life difficult for everyone else. They pity the abuser for having to live with such a selfish troublemaker. She is stigmatized wherever she goes.

Catherine Clark Kroeger, President Emerita, Christians for Biblical Equality:

Domestic violence ranks as the number one public health problem for women in America, and yet those of the cloth prefer to look the other way. They know, of course, that incidents do happen, but not in their congregation. Their folk are too nice, too spiritual, too well taught, too well balanced, too mature, too upstanding, and too discreet. A prime defense is to deny that the problem exists even though the evidence tells us that there is a strong likelihood of spousal abuse in every faith community.

If an admission must be made, pastors often minimize, conceal, or ignore the reality. Few dare to speak directly to the perpetrator about the problem. Many prefer to dodge so embarrassing and uncomfortable an issue. The truth is that they simply do not know what to do in abusive family situation. Many clergy persons have followed popular evangelical trends in idolizing and idealizing the family.

The bible, however, speaks forthrightly of troubled families and of God's redemptive work among them. Honesty, not silence, is the key to healing.... Although victims turn more often to their pastors than to all other resources combined, clergy and other pastoral ministers simply have not been equipped to meet the challenge. (44)

What happens when the church sides with the abuser.

Religious leaders are mostly esteemed in our society. When they respond to a disclosure of abuse with compassion and knowledge of the dynamics, it can be healing and life-saving to the victim and her children. However, when they side with patriarchal tradition, they not only re-victimize the wife, but they add spiritual abuse on top of the domestic abuse she is already burdened under.

Leaders may also feel they can take a neutral stance between the husband and wife. However, neutrality means siding with the abuser because they effectively say it is not abuse. Either way, it enables the abuser to continue, and accelerates the abuse.

Pastor Jeff Crippen:

Christian support/enabling of the abuser makes him conclude that God is on his side. That he is in the right. It makes him out to be a holy jihadist, zealous for the Lord, ready and willing to wipe out any opposition. Christians who enable abusers actually hand over the keys to a new and improved torture chamber to the evil man, and they do so in the name of the Lord! That is blasphemy. It is using the Lord's name in vain.

"... they have spoken in my name lying words that I did not command them. I am the one who knows, and I am witness, declares the LORD." (Jeremiah 29:23b)

What does this say about the culpability of Christians who enable the abuser? It says that they share in the guilt for this wickedness. They participate in the oppression of the victim. They have blood on their hands.

You see, while we are errant human beings, falling quite short of perfection, nevertheless there are some things we simply must get right... So, Christian, remember this and mark it down well. The next time you preach things like "just go back to him and submit and pray for him more" to victims, the next time you preach a sermon about how husbands are to be masters and priests in their home and how wives are to submit to them in all things, you are a participant in the abuse being dished out to the victim and in fact you are increasing its severity because you have endorsed the wicked man's thinking that he has God on his side.

God is most certainly not on the abuser's side, and furthermore, He is not on yours [errant clergy] either. (45)

Dr. Russell Moore, minister and author, instructs churches on how to respond to abusers:

Church discipline against wife-beaters must be clear and consistent. We must stand with women against predatory men in all areas of abandonment, divorce, and neglect. We must train up men, through godly mentoring as well as through biblical instruction, who will know that the model of a husband is a man who crucifies his selfish materialism, his libidinal fantasies, and his wrathful temper tantrums in order to care lovingly for a wife. We must also remind these young men that every idle word, and every hateful act, will be laid out in judgment before the eyes of the One to whom we must give an answer. (46)

Carol Adams, author of *When the Abuser Is Among Us: One Church's Response to a Perpetrator*, has this to say about a proper response by the church to disclosure of abuse:

> Accountability or collusion. I explained that in responding to the abuser it was essential to focus on behavior, not characteristics; otherwise we may succumb to the great temptation of identifying with the perpetrator and the perpetrator's pain instead of being focused on the victim's pain. Identification with him can mean that we feel anxiety over his being called to accountability and may prevent us from doing what he most needs. Within Christian communities there is often confusion about calling to accountability in that we think that being loving and Christlike is releasing someone from their sufferings, rather than saying, "I will be with you as you experience the consequences of your behavior." (47)

Pastor Jeff Crippen lays out practical guidelines to keep in mind if you are going to say anything to your church. Compare their response to what Pastor Jeff lays out as a proper response to you:

- Clergy will believe you. This is not blind acceptance but knowledge that "in most cases those who report abuse are speaking with honesty."
- They will not be influenced based on who the abuser is, understanding that all forms of abuse (not just physical or sexual) are serious.

- They will report abuse to police and allow the justice system to act.
- They will protect you from accusations.
- They will dissuade you from attempting to cover up the abuse.
- They will preach on the topic of abuse to prepare and protect the congregation.

As clergy deals with the abuser, they will:

- Question everything. Even "facts" he states with absolute confidence.
- Believe nothing without corroboration.
- Assume he is attempting to deceive them.
- Accept nothing less than full, unqualified repentance.
- Will not pity him, no matter how emotional he might be.
- Accept no excuses.
- Will not let him blame others. (48)

I hope this helps you as much as it helped me. The most important thing is to not take on the inevitable feelings of anger and bitterness you will feel if your church turns against you. Know with certainty that God is angry when people wound the afflicted in His name. They are not representing God at all. God is for you and will stand by you. Please do not turn away from Him because of the foolishness, selfishness and ignorance of people who claim to be representing Him. God will deal with them in His timing and wisdom. Instead, turn to God even more for comfort and a greater outpouring of His love and compassion in your life.

Speaking to leadership about red flags you see in your church.

This is something that comes up often with victims and I want to touch on it before leaving this subject of the church. When you have experienced abuse, it is easy to spot the signs of abuse elsewhere. If you are in a toxic church, you may see red flags of inappropriate behavior.

If you respectfully question (not accusing) something you see going on that you are uncomfortable with, you might be told that (a) you need counseling for even thinking of it; (b) that your experience has colored your judgment; (c) that you are the one with the problem; or (d) that you are the only one to have a problem with it.

In all likelihood, this is untrue. This is a brilliant way for toxic people to shift the attention off themselves and onto your supposed inadequacy and incompetence. Since you as a victim may have poor self-esteem, this ploy works well to get you off the trail if there is something inappropriate going on. Spiritual abuse signs are similar to domestic abuse signs. In this case, toxic leadership wants to get the attention off them and onto you. This is known as *blame-shifting*.

Telling a sexual abuse victim she is not qualified to recognize signs of sexual abuse because of her experience is like telling a firefighter he is not qualified to recognize signs of a fire because of his experience. It's absurd. BECAUSE of your experience, you are more qualified to notice red flags. If someone belittles you because you have experienced something, walk away with your head high. The question of credibility is on them, not on you. Take it as the sign it is of a toxic environment you need not be part of.

A proper response to your concerns would be to respectfully listen and assurance of looking into the matter further. Respect, not accusation, is the key word for both sides toward each other.

Abusers (and abusive churches) don't want you to value yourself and your experience. They want you to doubt yourself, shrink back and stay quiet. I want to validate you as a person who has gained wisdom and insight from your experience. You are not crazy or inferior.

It will take time, but as you heal, you will learn that your experience is valuable and there is no shame in what you have been through. Your voice matters. Everything you have been through will help someone else someday, so don't shrink back in shame. Speak up if you see something that concerns you. It may be life-saving for someone else. How others respond is between them and God. You can move on with your self-respect and integrity intact.

If you are witnessing abuse against children, or suspect it, don't just say something to leadership and then walk away. Turn to professionals outside of the church for advice and help. Police, advocates at your shelter or another professional agency can give you feedback on what you are seeing or sensing and give advice on what to do about it next.

Divorce

We have already established that God permits divorce in cases of malignant abuse. Since we know that God is more interested in our heart attitude, how can we be sure we have a right attitude towards biblically permissible divorce? Does it matter if a breach of covenant is a single act? Or is it an ongoing state of sin that qualifies one to pursue divorce?

For example, say you and your husband have been growing distant toward each other because of long work hours and a new baby. He has a single illicit encounter with the secretary at work. Biblically you have the right to leave the marriage. He breached your marriage covenant. But is this the best thing for you to do? Does it matter for you if it is an intermittent or isolated incident? Or is this encounter habitual?

At the least, the affair is a onetime error in judgment that possibly could be remedied. It could be a wake-up call for you as a couple to get help and find satisfying solutions for both of you. Could you forgive it and use it as a stepping-stone to a solid marriage? Is your husband genuinely grieved over it? In this case, ask the Lord if He wants you to attempt restoration and healing. It has happened to many women who are now grateful they didn't give up on their marriage. Seek God for that leading since He knows your husband's heart the best.

However, if you are dealing with a true abuser, this option is probably not possible. Abuse permeates every facet of life and sexual unfaithfulness is the norm rather than the exception. More than likely to him his infidelity is no big deal. He will feel entitled to it and even blame you for it, if not outright flaunting it in your face. He feels no remorse and has no genuine intention to change.

However the breach of covenant has taken place, your trust has been painfully trampled on. Trust is essential to a biblical marriage.

Barbara Roberts, author of *Not Under Bondage: Biblical Divorce for Abuse, Adultery and Desertion*, places the blame for the breach of covenant where it belongs, on the abuser:

> The perpetration of domestic abuse effectively pushes away the other spouse and divides the marriage. The fact that many victims eventually leave abusive relationships testifies to this pushing away. Perpetrators usually protest that they want the marriage to continue, but their evil conduct conveys the exact opposite—it effectually pushes the opposite spouse away.

> When applying 1 Corinthians 7:15, the key question is not "Who walked out?" but "Who caused the separation?" Would it be sensible to say that David was the sinful rebellious one when he left Saul's court? No, he left because of Saul's abuse. David left, but Saul was the cause of his leaving. If we translate the word chorizo as "separate" we see this more clearly: if the unbeliever separates, let him separate. The unbeliever is doing the separating; the believer is commanded to let it be done. This tells the believing spouse (and the church) to allow the marriage to be over, because the unbeliever has destroyed the covenant. It permits the victim of abuse to take out a legal divorce. Let there be chorizo = let there be separation = let there be legal divorce, because the word chorizo means both separation and divorce... (49)

What if the abuser is a professing Christian? Then an effort should be made to bring him to repentance, and this should be done through accountability to others such as the police, clergy and other professionals.

1 Corinthians 7:15 applies to marriages where the spouse is an unbeliever. If a professing Christian does not show genuine repentance, then according to the Bible, he should be treated as an unbeliever. The victim is then at liberty to get a divorce.

By the time a victim has come to the place of wondering about a divorce, she has already done a great deal to try to save the relationship. Grace and forgiveness to restore a relationship is possible where the erring partner genuinely repents. Premeditated chronic abuse, abandonment and abnormal behaviors are at minimum toxic, and usually terminal to a marriage covenant.

Whether or not you choose to end your marriage, it is essential you live your life with integrity and virtue anyway. Value and protect your relationship with the Lord above anyone and anything else.

If it is coming down to choosing whether to please God or please your husband, God must be first. He will honor you and help you through whatever you face.

God loves you, and He alone understands the depth of your heartache, fears, worries, confusion and all the obstacles you are facing. No matter where you are today, what mistakes you have made, what trials you are dealing with — you can start fresh with Him. He extends to you His love, grace and an opportunity to make a fresh start!

Don't accept criticism from anyone for a choice made between you and God. If you divorce, let no one beat you up about it. God views divorce as final (Deuteronomy 24:1-4). God is a God of fresh starts and wants to fill you with peace, forgiveness and love (1 Corinthians 7:15). Let God be your redeemer!

I left my husband and never regretted it. I worried about what the effects on the kids would be whether we stayed or whether we left. When I left, my daughters were 2, 4 and 5 years old so please take that into consideration with my story. I was willing to live with personal pain and trauma if it was better for the kids to remain in the home just for the sake of having a father. The few people I talked to gave strong opinions about it: stay no matter how bad it is so you don't deprive the kids of their dad; or get away and protect the children from witnessing and experiencing abuse. Both sides had a convincing argument for what they believed.

My final choice was to leave Brian to protect the girls from what I believed would be a dark future. To my knowledge, they had not been physically or sexually abused yet, but since all the signs were pointing to imminent violation, I got out before it could take place.

I didn't leave with any intention of getting a divorce. I left out of fear for my kids and needing to get away from the environment so I could think things through. It didn't make sense how valuable an abusive father could be to them. I knew many kids who had grown up without fathers and were mature happy adults. They enjoyed healthy interpersonal relationships because they had one healthy parent who loved them.

In hindsight, I can hardly believe I ever had difficulty making the choice to leave. Unfortunately, when a victim is in an abusive environment, nothing makes clear sense. Everything is muddled and confusing. That's why getting away from the environment and influence of the abuser can make a world of difference in gaining clarity. Add insight from outsiders, particularly advocates trained in recognizing the signs of abuse, and you can make progress in understanding what is happening and how you need to respond.

My decision to leave was the right one. To my surprise, all three of my daughters thanked me for getting them away from daddy and made me promise they would never have to go back to him. One of my daughters prayed this prayer within a week of us leaving Brian: "Dear God, thank you for getting us away from daddy. I want You to live in my heart forever because now I know that You love us because You got us away from daddy."

That prayer came from a child who I thought was unaware of what was going on since there was no physical violence against us. My daughters never looked back after we left. They jumped into their new life full-speed with joy and energy. They developed friendships with wonderful people and began to heal, grow and thrive. My girls love the Lord, love school, have healthy relationships and support, and are growing in their unique gifts.

I share this to encourage you that kids know a lot more about what is going on than we think they do. If we provide them with safety, security and a ton of love, they can flourish without living all the time with an abusive parent. Kids are resilient, and we can nurture their resiliency by listening to them and giving them a safe environment to grow up in. Exposure to abuse puts kids at risk, but we can counteract that with our unconditional love and a supportive network.

In case you are wondering, I filed for a divorce a year after leaving. Brian threatened many horrible things and I was sick over the thought of what would happen if he was allowed to be alone with the girls. But the judge recognized the danger and ruled to completely protect the girls from him. Brian then disappeared from our lives.

Not every case turns out that well. I know that many of you reading this have already lost custody of your children to your abuser. You have my greatest compassion and prayers. I only offer my experience to show that if you think you have to stay because your kids need to have their father full-time, that is not necessarily true. They will do better not being in a toxic environment even if only for short breaks.

Whether you stay or leave is something only you can decide. It is never a simple decision to make and most people do not understand the difficult dynamics surrounding the issue. To leave successfully may take months of planning and preparing. Or it may be something you do overnight with no preparation because you don't have a choice in it. Don't let people who don't understand your situation place guilt trips on you. Those of us who have been down this road know all too well the hardship that accompanies it, and few outsiders comprehend it. When they say things, take what is helpful and leave the rest behind.

In the next chapter, we will look at what our response to abusers should be. God wants us to respond to abusers rightly, but what does that look like? You may not even need to know because you've decided to get out and be done with it. But if you have children together or you decide to stay with him longer, you will have to deal with him. We will look at forgiveness and grief, and the signs of true repentance and change.

Reflection: Decision-Making

Decision-making. It's one of the most important skills to have, yet most of us are never taught it. A bad decision can cost dearly, but the only true failure is if we don't learn and grow from it.

Earlier we talked about your values helping you define your boundaries. Your values are also your guide to making decisions that direct you toward your goals. If you haven't yet, do the Values Exercise (A) and write down your top five values on an index card you can keep with you.

Knowing your values lessens the confusion and fear of decision-making. Your values create clarity and simplify the process. When a new opportunity presents itself, or change is necessary, ask yourself:

- Does this opportunity meet my values?
- Will this take me closer to my goals?

If your answer to those are "no" then the decision is already made. Even when it's difficult and risky, stay true to your values and your decisions will feel more peaceful and authentic. The outcome will be better than if you compromised your values.

If you are in a controlling relationship, you may not be allowed to make decisions. It can be scary to take on the responsibility, but you can do it and it will feel great to discover you can trust yourself to make good choices. Better yet, you are resourceful and will recover if you make a mistake. It's rare for a mistake to be permanent. Sometimes what seems like a mistake at first will be the catalyst to something unexpectedly good.

Recall my story about being stranded on the beach. I realized

I could not allow Brian to continue making all of our decisions. I wasn't used to taking an active role in making decisions, especially ones that would affect our future. It wasn't like I could gradually work up to it either. No, I had to make life-altering decisions right then. I did it, trusting God to guide me, and it all worked out well. The journey was crazy though! I still made mistakes but worked through them until I was back on course.

It's okay for your spouse to decide things as long as it's also your choice and you're happy with the direction your life is heading. However, it's not okay if your life is being detrimentally controlled. Either way, you must recognize where you are not in control or part of the decision-making process. Decide whether this is in your best interest or in the best interest of him or others.

- How often do you make decisions?
- What decisions are you allowing someone else to make for you?
- What is significant about these decisions?
- How are these decisions affecting your life?
- How are your children affected?
- Could you make these decisions yourself?
- Should you be making these decisions yourself?
- What are the implications if you don't make a decision?

If you need to decide something, but are paralyzed by fear of making the wrong choice, use these questions and the process below to gain clarity:

- What are your needs, priorities and objectives in this situation?
- What do you need to achieve this objective?
- What would you like to do if you knew you couldn't fail?

- How must you prioritize your efforts?
- What's available to help you make the best possible decision in this situation?
- What decision will allow for new opportunities?
- What will your decision cost in terms of time and personal resources?
- What is the cost if you decide not to go through with this?
- What sacrifices might you need to make?
- Are other people pressuring you a certain way?
- What impact does this pressure have on you?
- What emotions are influencing your perspective of this situation?
- Is this likely to be a rational or emotional decision?
- What are you afraid of?
- What is your intuition telling you to do?

Effective decision-making requires flexibility, curiosity and at times courage. Having a process to work through helps us rationally think things through. Below is a simple process that will guide you. Be sure to write down your answers.

> *"The most difficult thing is the decision to act, the rest is merely tenacity. The fears are paper tigers. You can do anything you decide to do. You can act to change and control your life; and the procedure, the process is its own reward."*
>
> ~ Amelia Earhart

Tips for Effective Decision-Making

1. Identify the decision that must be made.
2. Research your options.
3. Research potential outcomes associated with each option.
4. Seek objective opinions from others you trust.
5. Commit yourself to making your decision.
6. Monitor your progress and results.
7. If you hit a snag, start through the process again until you are okay with the results.

"In any moment of decision, the best thing you can do is the right thing, the next best thing is the wrong thing, and the worst thing you can do is nothing."

~ Theodore Roosevelt

Foundation

"Your word is a lamp to my feet, And a light to my path."

Psalm 119:105 (AMP)

"Where there is no [wise, intelligent] guidance, the people fall [and go off course like a ship without a helm], But in the abundance of [wise and godly] counselors there is victory."

Proverbs 11:14 (AMP)

"Who are they that live in the holy fear of God? You will show them the right path to take."

Psalm 25:12 (TPT)

Chapter 14

A Biblical Response to Abuse

WHILE I ENDURED an unhappy marriage, I often wondered how God expected me to respond beyond submission and prayer. I was sure I wasn't supposed to violate God's moral law, but felt a conflict because Brian often did.

It's not a conflict when we find out what God wants. We experience conflict when we don't understand God's will, which He revealed in His Word. That's why it is so important to study the Bible, rather than just accepting what people (even a husband and clergy) claim about it.

One thing God is clear about is that our loyalty and love must go to Him first before anyone and anything else.

> *"'Teacher, which commandment in the law is the greatest?' He [Jesus] said to him, 'You shall love the Lord your God with all your heart, and with all your soul, and with all your mind.' This is the greatest and first commandment. And a second is like it: 'You shall love your neighbor as yourself.' On these two commandments hang all the law and the prophets."*
>
> Matthew 22:36-40

Jesus did NOT say wives shall love their husbands with all their heart, soul and mind. He said we are to love Him first with everything we are!

When we elevate God to His rightful place above our husband, then confusion will lose its grip on us. 1 Corinthians 14:33 says God is not a God of confusion and disorder but of peace and order. Confusion and disorder define abusive relationships, so if the source of that is not God, then we know that the enemy of our souls is the source.

God is against injustice and the abuse of power. It doesn't matter where this is taking place, whether in a country, a community, a church, a home or a marriage.

> *"He has told you, O mortal, what is good; and what does the Lord require of you but to do justice, and to love kindness, and to walk humbly with your God?"*
>
> Micah 6:8

When we face the sin of abuse, it is tempting to react with a sinful response of our own. That may be with compromise, passiveness or overt anger in any number of ways. Please remember I am speaking in general. Sometimes being passive is important for safety. I'm referring to an attitude toward abuse where passivity means hopeless acceptance.

Romans 12:21 says, *"Do not be overcome by evil, but overcome evil with good."* 1 Peter 3:9, *"Do not repay evil for evil or abuse for abuse; but, on the contrary, repay with a blessing. It is for this that you were called—that you might inherit a blessing."* This shows a proactive approach toward abuse.

Other places in the Bible talk about using wisdom in our dealings such as Ephesians 5:15-17, *"Be careful then how you live, not as unwise people but as wise, making the most of the time, because the days are evil. So do not be foolish, but understand what the will of the Lord is."*

Jeremiah 9:24 further reveals God's heart: *"but let those who boast, boast in this, that they understand and know me, that I am the Lord; I act with steadfast love, justice and righteousness in the earth, for in these things I delight, says the Lord."*

Some moral dilemmas I faced with Brian were things like him wanting me to take drugs with him or selling things he stole from work. If I suspected he was cheating on me, should I keep my mouth shut or confront him? If he wanted to drive the kids somewhere while he was drunk, do I say no or cave to avoid a fight and just pray for their protection? If a man wants to visit with me, is that okay since I'm not getting attention from my husband? How much lying should I do for him? Where is the boundary between having a clear conscience with God and submitting to my husband for the sake of peace? The dilemmas progressed, just as all abuse progresses in intensity and methods.

The Bible says we cannot serve two masters: *"Am I now seeking human approval, or God's approval? Or am I trying to please people? If I were still pleasing people, I would not be a servant of Christ."* (Galatians 1:10)

When we find ourselves in an abusive relationship, God wants us to respond with love and wisdom, and stand for justice and righteousness. Not only are we to do this for ourselves, but we are to do it for others who we see being oppressed. When there is a moral conflict between our husband or God, then God's way always overrules man's.

Responding with abusive behavior or speech when we are provoked only makes things worse. If that was justified for us as victims, then abusive behavior by perpetrators would be justified. People will provoke us in many situations and relationships throughout life. As lovers of Christ and carriers of His nature, we are to take the high road.

For those who think there is a cut and dried response in an abusive relationship, there isn't. Often victims, knowing a violent episode is on its way, will provoke it to get it over with as a matter of self-preservation. There is no condemnation to anyone in these dangerous situations. However, once we know that God does not want us to live under these circumstances, it frees us to explore alternatives.

God will give you wisdom to know when and how to stand for truth and righteousness. He will not demand you to do something that puts you in harm's way. What matters is coming into agreement with His will and seeking Him for how to live that out in your present circumstances.

God wants us to protect ourselves

Along with the principle of siding with truth and righteousness, is coming under protection. This is a biblical principle and not one you need to feel is contrary to God's will for you.

> *"My heart is in anguish within me, the terrors of death have fallen upon me. Fear and trembling come upon me, and horror overwhelms me. And I say, "O that I had wings like a dove! I would fly away and be at rest; truly, I would flee far away; I would lodge in the wilderness; I would hurry to find a shelter for myself from the raging wind and tempest."*
>
> Psalms 55:4-8

Do you ever feel like that? I remember a time like that about a month before I fled from Brian with the girls. I laid face down in a muddy pasture broken and done for. I longed for the comfort of death. I didn't think I could take one more second of the anguish and fear. Sometimes the wisest thing to do is to remove yourself from a dangerous situation, at least temporarily.

Here are verses showing how much God loves you and wants you to be safe. Sometimes God does miraculously deliver us from harm, but often we need to use wisdom and run from it knowing God is with us and will help us!

"The clever see danger and hide; but the simple go on, and suffer for it."

Proverbs 22:3

"For the protection of wisdom is like the protection of money, and the advantage of knowledge is that wisdom gives life to the one who possesses it."

Ecclesiastics 7:12

"The angel of the Lord encamps around those who fear Him, and delivers them."

Psalm 34:7

"You are a hiding place for me; you preserve me from trouble; you surround me with glad cries of deliverance. Selah."

Psalm 32:7

"When the righteous cry for help, the LORD hears, and rescues them from all their troubles. The Lord is near to the brokenhearted, and saves the crushed

in spirit. Many are the afflictions of the righteous, but the LORD rescues them from them all."

Psalm 34:17-19

"But let all who take refuge in you rejoice; let them ever sing for joy. Spread your protection over them, so that those who love your name may exult in you."

Psalm 5:11

"The Lord helps them and rescues them; He rescues them from the wicked, and saves them, because they take refuge in Him."

Psalm 37:40

You are valued and precious in God's eyes! He does not want men who do not appreciate your worth to hurt you. Being married to an abusive man does not mean you have to take whatever he dishes out to you. As we learned earlier, if your husband is violent toward you, HE has already broken the marriage covenant. God does not ask you to continue to submit to that evil.

1 Corinthians 3:16-17 says God considers you his temple: *"Do you not know that you are God's temple and that God's Spirit dwells in you? If anyone destroys God's temple, God will destroy that person. For God's temple is holy, and you are that temple."*

"The thief comes only to steal and kill and destroy. I came that they may have life, and have it abundantly."

John 10:10

God wants you to live an abundant life. Is there room for fear and abuse in an abundant life? Abundant life includes feeling safe, loved and respected.

God wants us to protect our children

Jesus treated children with love, kindness, care and protection. In no way did Jesus ever abuse a child or condone it. There is never any justification for harshness toward children. Often Proverbs 13:24 (spare the rod, spoil the child) is misused to justify abusive behavior towards kids, but that is not what God intended. Love does not hurt!

The point of this verse is to encourage discipline as in guiding with love and kindness. In the Bible, shepherds used the rod to protect and guide the sheep, or to pull them out of dangerous places. They never used it to hurt them. That's why the psalmist in Psalm 23 references the rod as comforting: *"Your rod and Your staff - they comfort me."*

God expects us as moms to take our role seriously as protectors of our children. It is NEVER okay to turn a blind eye to children suffering abuse. Of all people, moms must be there to protect and nurture the children, even if we must sacrifice our own comfort to do it.

Not that our efforts to protect our children are always successful, but we have to try our best and leave what we can't control in the Lord's hands. If you feel you can't stand up for your child out of fear of the consequences by the abuser, then it's time to reconsider staying in that relationship.

I like the website, *The Mama Bear Effect*. While they primarily address child sexual abuse, their tips on deterring abuse applies for protecting children from any kind of abuse, including from family members. I will paraphrase their article, but visiting the website and reading the whole article is worth it:

- Show that you are a loving and attentive parent. Be involved in your child's life! It sends an important message to your child that they are valued, and it sends a message to abusers (including fathers) that abuse of the child is not going to be accepted.

- Trust yourself over others and speak up if something doesn't feel right. Your instincts protect you and your child from danger, so if something doesn't feel right, have the courage to say no to it. Assuming your abusive husband has your child's best interests in mind is a mistake. If your husband doesn't have the integrity to treat you right, he doesn't have the integrity to treat anyone right, least of all the most vulnerable. If he cared about the child, he would love and respect the child's mother.

- Respect and listen to your child. If your child knows you value their feelings and opinions, they are more likely to tell you what's going on when they are being hurt.

- Be someone who is knowledgeable about child abuse and speaks up about it.

- Raise your child to have faith in their self-worth and right to respect, and let others know you have taught your children. (50)

An abusive spouse is also often abusing the children. If they aren't blatantly hurting them, they may flood the child with attention and gifts to alienate them from you. This is also a form of abuse. Read Appendix B about signs of an abusive parent.

There are no guarantees that trying to save your children will work since the legal system sometimes hinders a mother's ability to do that. But on a spiritual level, if you will honor God by doing what you can to protect your kids, God will honor your heart and your efforts and He can do what we as parents can't. Pray for your children daily, love them know matter how tough it gets, and stand up for them. Trust God to do what you cannot. He cares about them even more than you do, and when we as moms come into partnership with Him, good things happen.

When we have failed in the past, we can beat ourselves up and feel we can never make up for it. The times I feel the worst is when I acutely know of my shortcomings as a parent. The enemy loves to torment us with accusations in this area.

God is not accusing you though. Satan is the accuser. Whatever has happened in the past, God will forgive and let you start fresh today. Start today to find ways to support your kids. That may mean leaving your abuser and taking them to a safe house while you figure things out. Safe houses have good programs for kids to help them deal with their pain. It may mean turning your abuser in for what he has perpetrated against you and your children. It can mean many things. You need to listen to your heart and make sure your children have priority over any man in your life. While they are dependent, their needs come first. And the first need a child has is for safety: physically, sexually, emotionally and spiritually.

Whether to stay or leave for the sake of the children isn't always easy to make though. There are dynamics at play that only you know about although many will judge you if you feel that staying with the abuser is in your children's best interest.

Lundy Bancroft has this to say about mom's who stay with their abuser:

> There's no easy answer for the abused mother. Children don't want to lose their father, they just want his abusiveness and violence to stop. If she leaves him, she also faces economic hardships that could drag her away from her children - she might have to start working full time, for example, which could be a big loss for her and her kids if that wasn't the case

before. Children who are living with an abuser in their lives NEED THEIR MOTHERS.

And what if leaving him would actually mean she has less time to spend with the kids? It's hard to say if that's best. And then, the abuser is going to get visitation time, so suddenly the kids will be away from her whole weekends, half the day on their birthdays, half the day on holidays including the big religious holidays, and so forth. And finally, when his visitation starts, he's suddenly getting all this time alone with them where she has no way to keep an eye on what he's doing with them. So I think there are good reasons to leave and good reasons to stay, and we really need to respect the choices mothers make in these horrible binds. (51)

There are many supportive communities online that can help you navigate this, especially your fear of losing them if you stand up to the abuse, or how to deal with it if you have lost custody. It's one of the toughest things you will face, but God is greater. Put Him first, seek His wisdom, pray for your children daily and surround yourself with people who can support you because they have been through it too.

I have listed in the Resources some websites that offer good information and support on this subject. There are also many programs available to help mothers be independent so they are less likely to stay in unhealthy relationships. Programs may assist with childcare, education, job opportunities, parenting skills, and financial support and literacy. You can call the *National Domestic Violence Hotline* at 1-800-799-7233 for your local resources.

Seek help from higher authorities

One of the primary environments abuse of any kind must have to flourish is secrecy. Exposing abuse to the light is the only way for both victims and abusers to get help. Ephesians 5:11 says, *"Take no part in the unfruitful works of darkness, but instead expose them."*

The purpose of exposing abuse is clear in James 5:19-20, *"My brothers and sisters, if anyone among you wanders from the truth and is brought back by another, you should know that whoever brings back a sinner from wandering will save the sinner's soul from death and will cover a multitude of sins."*

It is biblical to seek help from higher authorities when you are experiencing abuse. It is biblical to flee to a shelter or to talk to the police. God put the law into place to protect victims. Domestic violence is against the law, including marital rape. Police or domestic violence agencies can talk to you about the laws in your state that can protect you.

> *"Let every person be subject to the governing authorities; for there is no authority except from God, and those authorities that exist have been instituted by God. Therefore whoever resists authority resists what God has appointed, and those who resist will incur judgment. For rulers are not a terror to good conduct, but to bad. Do you wish to have no fear of the authority? Then do what is good, and you will receive its approval; for it is God's servant for your good. But if you do what is wrong, you should be afraid, for the authority does not bear the sword in vain! It is the servant of God to execute wrath on the wrongdoer. Therefore one must be subject, not only because of wrath but also because of conscience."*
>
> Romans 13:1-5

Leslie Vernick says this about responding to abuse:

- It is good to protect yourself (Proverbs 27:12; Proverbs 11:9). David fled King Saul when he was violent toward him. The angel of the Lord warned Joseph to flee to Egypt with Jesus because Herod was trying to kill him. Paul escaped from those who sought to stone him. If you are being mistreated, and you have tried speaking up, standing up and setting boundaries and nothing has changed or stopped the abusive behavior, I believe it is biblically permissible to separate yourself from the abusive person in order to protect yourself from further harm.

- It is good to expose the abuser (Ephesians 5:11) Sometimes we're very afraid to be bold and take a stand because then it lets other's know that our marriage is a mess and our spouse has been abusive. Bringing this out into the open is the ONLY way to get help for both yourself as well as your spouse. When things remain hidden, then a person can more easily stay self-deceived and blind to his/her own brokenness.

Also it is important to ask yourself if there is anything that you are doing to provoke and/or escalate a difficult or volatile situation. I have worked with couples where one spouse is trying to shut the conflict down because he or she is afraid of losing control, but the other spouse will not stop their arguing. The situation escalates and the one who feared losing control, does. I'm not excusing the abusive person in these cases, but sometimes we do create a situation where it is harder for someone to handle themselves in a godly way.

- It is good to allow the violent person to experience the consequences of his/her sinful behavior. One of life's greatest teachers is consequences. God says what we sow, we reap (Galatians 6:7). A person uses violence at home because they can. God has put the civil authorities in place to protect victims of abuse. The apostle Paul appealed to the Roman government when he was being mistreated (Acts 22:24-29).

When someone continually mistreats us, they lose the fellowship of our company. God does not ask us to have unconditional relationships with people even as He asks us to unconditionally love them. He calls us to love our enemies, not necessarily have fellowship with him/her. In a marital relationship what that means is that you will act in your spouses' best interests, even when that is difficult and costs you. (52)

Response to People Blaming You

One thing you may encounter and may sound reasonable is a version of this: "You are the one making him treat you this way. You are the one to blame. He wouldn't treat you like this if you weren't so ___."

This is what Lundy Bancroft says in response to a question during an interview with *Pandora's Project* about victim blaming:

> Kate: I have been told by therapists and also read (especially Dr Phil; but even Maya Angelou) that we teach people how to treat us. If this is true, how much of this is my fault? By staying wasn't I teaching the person that it was ok to continually treat me this way

> LundyBancroft: These people are confusing abusers with other people. You can't significantly change an abuser's behavior. Leaving him is sometimes the best decision for you - that's a decision only you can make - but he will usually move on to find another woman to abuse. Maybe if a whole series of women leave him he'll start to change a little, but it tends to take more than that to make an abuser change—it

tends to take arrest, prosecution, an abuser program, and (according to the research) a spell in jail.

I'm sorry that those kinds of woman-blaming and victim-blaming theories get so much air time in the media. Women do need to find ways to take more power, but the path to power isn't by blaming yourself for falling in a trap that someone else had no business setting in the first place. I would also want to say to Dr. Phil, and to Maya Angelou, "You, and all community members, contribute a lot to making it possible for abusers to get away with what they do, then you blame women for what happens.

If abused women share part of the responsibility, then their communities share even more of the responsibility for harboring abusers, letting them off the hook, buying into their excuses, supporting their mentality, and so forth. I don't think Dr. Phil and Maya Angelou would be so open to looking at THEIR contribution to the problem, would they? But they are happy to say that you should look at yours. As far as I'm concerned, the victims of a social tragedy are not the ones that should be assigned the primary responsibility to fix it. (53)

When you encounter victim blaming, a good response is to counter it with truth:

- Abuse is a conscious choice made by the abuser. They could walk away or communicate respectfully.
- Abuse is not about how the abuser was incited to hurt the victim, but rather feeling he is entitled to do what he wants to the victim.
- Reframe questions away from "why does the victim..." to "why does the perpetrator abuse?"

Response to His Claimed Repentance (signs it's authentic)

Developing new habits and new thinking patterns takes time to take root and show itself to be genuine. It will rarely be instant and lasting. Many abusers, if it suits their interests, can put on the appearance of being a new person for two or three years or more. Even if he claims a miraculous encounter with God that has changed him, remain skeptical and let time (a lot of time) tell the truth.

That does not mean you doubt God, but you are wise and cautious. God doesn't normally change a person's basic character and personality. Yes, He delivers and sets free, but it will still take time and effort to overcome old ways of thinking and behaving — old patterns and habits don't just go away overnight.

Sometimes Brian would get remorseful and declare that "As of this moment, I am a changed man! I will never let Satan into my life again. Never!" He would expect me to forget all his bad behavior and be thrilled that from then on he would "be the man of my dreams."

If he meant it when he said it, he did not put forth the effort toward change when the drama of the moment was over. The next few hours or days, as his enthusiasm faded, he went right back to his old ways. He would tell me to "be thankful I'm not like other men." (This shows the abuse cycle is still happening.)

Signs he isn't changing:

Lundy Bancroft offers these signs that your abuser is not changing:

- He tells you that you should be appreciating how much he has changed.

- He says "I can't be perfect" as an excuse to keep doing abusive things.

- He thinks it's okay to keep being abusive, as long as the incidents are farther apart than they used to be. (e.g. he says,

"You are so upset with me, and I haven't done anything like that in a long time - I've been really good.")

- He tells you that now it's time for you to focus on the changes that you need to make.

- He is disconnecting from you emotionally - in other words, the reason he is being less abusive is that he is simply not being anything very much—he's withdrawn.

- He is continuing to make excuses.

- He says "We're getting along better." which means that as soon as you start to stand up to him or challenge him forcefully again, he'll be going right back to his old ways.

- He still gets impatient when you try to talk to him in a serious way about the things that are really important to you in life, including your desires for the relationship. (54)

Evidence of authentic change:

- He accepts responsibility for his choice to abuse you and acknowledges that the abuse is wrong no matter what. That means no more excuses and blaming you or others for it.

- He understands and accepts that you are not his property and he does not have the right to control and dominate you. (This may be impossible if he believes that God has made him master over you - tough to give up that lofty position!)

- He listens to, considers and respects your opinion even if he doesn't agree with it, and you feel safe to respectfully disagree with his. (For example, I wanted furniture in our house rather than sitting on the floor. When Brian got tax-refund money, I asked him if we could purchase an attractive used living room set I had found on Craig's List. He pretended to listen and agree, but the next day bought a Holstein cow for me to milk because it fondly reminded him of the cows he had milked in prison. This is NOT showing respect or care!)

- He doesn't demand an "Atta boy!" every time he behaves well. (Brian's ego had to be constantly stroked which exhausted me, and his good behavior was short-lived anyway so not genuine change.)

- He will also not treat every good instance as a voucher to be spent on an occasional act of abuse: "I've been really good for a long time, why are you making such a big deal about it?"

- He stops coercing or forcing you to have sex. He shows consideration for your needs and desires and respects your right to say "no."

- He will accept the natural consequences of his actions without blaming you, the children, others, or feeling sorry for himself. He also won't demand you fix it.

- He will change his response in heated environments. Whether it's another driver on the road, or your own frustration and anger, he will curb his own angry response.

- He will attempt to identify patterns and attitudes that drive his abuse and try to reduce or eliminate the triggers. As his wife, you will have good insight into this and he should ask for your perspective on what triggers him and not blow up at you for your insight.

- He understands that developing new thinking is a process he will have to continually work on—it will not be instant. If it is 'instant', then you are still stuck in the cycle of abuse. But if it is genuine, then even when he falls, he will take responsibility, make amends, and do what he has to do to make things right with you and the children.

- He won't use his 'change' as a bargaining chip to control you: "I did this, so now it's time for you to do…"
- He will make an effort to carry his weight and share the power in the home.
- He will improve his parenting, his treatment of you as a parent, and will adjust his overall attitude toward all females to be respectful.

Does this sound lofty and out of reach? This is actually how normal healthy people act most of the time. Continual self-growth and consideration of others is normal. Abuse is not. If your husband is being genuine, it will become clear over time. Anyone can claim whatever they want and even convince themselves of it. But only time, and subsequent actions when the pressure is on, will prove the veracity. If he gets angry at you for not being thrilled and convinced by his good behavior after the first two or three good episodes, then he has NOT changed! You are still stuck in the cycle of abuse.

Pastor Jeff Crippen shows us from the Bible what genuine change looks like from the life of Saul of Tarsus:

> But Christ can transform the chief of sinners—just as He laid hold of the murdering, persecuting Saul of Tarsus [Acts 9:1-9]. What will it look like? That is to say, what will happen—what will it look like—when an abuser is brought to genuine repentance? It will be traumatic—like no other trauma the man has probably ever experienced. When the bright, brilliant, penetrating and blinding light of Christ shines on him, such a man is going to suffer the trauma of realizing that everything he has been, all that he has thought, every goal he has pursued—the very grid and mindset through which he has perceived himself, other people, his victims, and God—ALL of it has been wrong! Radically, radically wrong. His mindset of

power and control, of entitlement and of justification is going to come crashing down as Christ shows him his nothingness.

Consider again how this trauma of repentance evidenced itself in Paul—*"But Saul, still breathing threats and murder against the disciples of the Lord, went to the high priest 2 and asked him for letters to the synagogues at Damascus, so that if he found any belonging to the Way, men or women, he might bring them bound to Jerusalem. 3 Now as he went on his way, he approached Damascus, and suddenly a light from heaven shone around him. 4 And falling to the ground he heard a voice saying to him, "Saul, Saul, why are you persecuting me?" 5 And he said, "Who are you, Lord?" And He said, "I am Jesus, whom you are persecuting. 6 But rise and enter the city, and you will be told what you are to do." 7 The men who were traveling with him stood speechless, hearing the voice but seeing no one. 8 Saul rose from the ground, and although his eyes were opened, he saw nothing. So they led him by the hand and brought him into Damascus. 9 And for three days he was without sight, and neither ate nor drank."* (Acts 9:1-9 ESV)

And THAT is how it will be for the abusive man who is brought to true repentance in Christ. This is why we can be assured that the truly repentant man will cease from ALL blaming of others, he will cease from making excuses, he will be done with insisting on anything from others, including forgiveness, he will be entirely through with minimizing his sin, and he, who for his entire life viewed himself as a master, will now be humbled in the dust and become the slave of Christ and the servant of others. Where these changes are absent, there is NO real repentance. (55)

Reflection: Expectations

Expectations. Our biggest frustrations and heartache are often the result of misplaced expectations of others. Identifying and changing our expectations will reduce unnecessary suffering and help to refocus on things that matter. People rarely behave the way we want them to. Hope for the best, but expect less!

Acceptance however, reduces conflict and increases our satisfaction with life. By asking the below questions, we can realize what we can and cannot change. Think about one expectation you have right now. Answer the questions to create self-awareness of expectation versus acceptance:

- Where does your expectation come from?
- How is this expectation serving you?
- What does acceptance mean to you?
- How do you feel when you accept the reality?
- What's the worst that can happen if you let go of your expectation and accept reality?

Tips for Removing Misplaced Expectations

- What other people think doesn't matter

You are not here to live up to other people's expectations and demands. This includes an unreasonable and toxic spouse. Do you feel good about your own desires and decisions? The more you approve of your choices, the less approval you need from others. Be yourself and listen to your intuition. What other people think doesn't matter. True strength is about having faith and trust in who you are and a willingness to act upon it.

- Don't beg anyone for love and respect

When you practice self-love and self-respect, you give yourself the opportunity to grow and be happy. If you change, change because you want to and it makes you a better person. If you believe in something, fight for it. Great strength comes from knowing what you believe in and want, and standing up for it.

- Let other people be themselves

Stop expecting people to fit your idea of who they are. Allow them to be themselves and pay attention to what that is in reality. No excuses. No justifications. Tweak your expectations as needed. If your husband says he loves you, yet flirts with other women when you two go out, it's time to let go of your expectation. You can communicate how his flirting makes you feel, but if he doesn't respect that, then adjust your expectation of how he will act and make choices accordingly.

- Communicate

No one can read your mind. It's important to communicate how you feel and what you want. Clear communication may clear up simple misunderstandings.

- Stop hoping for change

If there's a specific behavior you're hoping disappears over time, you will be disappointed. You can't change people and you shouldn't try. Either accept who they are or live without them. Don't take it personally. People don't do things because of you, they do things because of them.

As a Christian, you are not responsible to change anyone or to pray them into change. A beautiful thing about God's design for us is the freedom to choose. Maybe the person will someday realize their error and put in the work to change, but that is not on you to force. Know when it's time to let go and surrender this person to the Lord's care while you move on.

Foundation

"The hope of the righteous ends in gladness, but the expectation of the wicked comes to nothing."

Proverbs 10:28

"Don't allow the actions of evil men to cause you to burn with anger. Instead, burn with unrelenting passion as you worship God in holy awe. Your future is bright and filled with a living hope that will never fade away. As you listen to me, my beloved child, you will grow in wisdom and your heart will be drawn into understanding, which will empower you to make right decisions."

Proverbs 23:17-19 (TPT)

"So above all, constantly chase after the realm of God's kingdom and the righteousness that proceeds from Him. Then all these less important things will be given to you abundantly."

Matthew 6:33 (TPT)

Chapter 15

Grief and Forgiveness

Grief

AS A RELATIONSHIP ends, we must accept grief as a normal part of the process of moving on to a better life. Long before I ever left Brian, I grieved the loss of my dreams of a happy life with him; losing the wonderful man I thought was the real him; and losing a loving dad for my daughters. I grieved the loss of other relationships and friendships; losing well-loved pets; losing my peace and joy. Through it, I didn't understand I was grieving, and that it was normal. All I knew was that the ache in my heart was deep and painful, relieved by spurts of happiness with Brian when he was remorseful.

After I left, I needed to grieve the loss of the relationship through separation and divorce, but the stress of trying to survive without Brian allowed no time for it. I stayed on edge and stressed out. Thank God for people who stepped in and encouraged me to take time for myself. This is one reason it is good to allow yourself to be open with others, such as in a dv support group. You will find allies and friends and you can encourage and help each other.

According to the Women's Resource Service in an article *Grief and Loss after Abuse*:

> When a woman leaves an abusive relationship, family and friends will often celebrate the strength and courage it has taken for her to end the relationship. They are often genuinely relieved that she and the children are safer and respond positively to her new life without him. Research shows that friends and family are less likely, however, to recognize the grief or loss a woman may also experience when a relationship ends, even though it has been abusive.
>
> These losses may include:
> - Loss of a home and familiar environment
> - Loss of a partner who (usually) she once loved
> - Loss of the dream of a safe, respectful and loving partner
> - Loss of security, financial or emotional
> - Loss of a normal or desired family unit for children
> - Loss of a sense of identity, and/or their self-belief
> - Loss of relationships with family members of the ex-partner
> - Loss of their own good judgment capacities given that they are often held responsible for the abuse they endured.
>
> This sense of loss can lead to feelings of intense grief. Although it is normal and natural, the process of grieving is quite hard and requires time, courage and support. (56)

Please allow yourself the right and the time to grieve your loss. There is nothing wrong with you and whatever you are feeling is legitimate. You don't have to apologize for it or explain yourself to anyone. It is an important stage to go through to move on to a healthy place. It helped me to join a support group. Even though I wasn't even considering a divorce when I joined, I was drawn to a Christian divorce support group (DivorceCare) and found an invaluable group of people who accepted me and journeyed with me.

I would like to add here that many women turn to the Church for support. Perhaps it will work for you, but as we talked about earlier, the Church often blames the victim for what happened. This only adds spiritual abuse on top of everything else you are going through. Your ex may even attend and turn everyone against you.

However, many churches are getting trained in domestic violence and facilitating safe domestic violence support groups for victims and survivors. If you are looking for spiritual support along with dv support, then these groups may be just what you are looking for. Ask around to see if anyone knows of such a group in your area. You can also call churches and ask if they have a "domestic violence support group."

Talk to your local shelter about dv support groups offered through them. Then you will know you are in a safe place where you can process at a comfortable pace and not fear judgment and condemnation. You might also ask them if they know of the church you are considering and if it has a reputation of blaming or supporting victims.

Also important is to be honest with others about what you are going through. This honors yourself and what you have experienced. People may not always respond helpfully, but by standing in truth you will gain strength. You do not have to be ashamed. Your abuser should be ashamed. Don't take on his guilt for him. Hold him accountable for his choices.

Something else I did was to hold a private funeral to commemorate the loss of my dreams and my relationship. It was just between

God and me, but it was powerful to acknowledge the death of something significant in my life. I parted with the ring that symbolized that relationship. I had also written a list of all the things I was struggling with. So much heartache poured out in that list but I buried it with the ring. After a lot of tears and talking to God about it all, I left that "funeral" feeling cleansed and more ready to face the future. I continued to grieve — it is a process that can take a long time, but the finality of that "funeral" was an important part of my healing.

Another thing that helps the grieving process is the awareness that losing a "normal" relationship and losing an "abusive" relationship are two different things. You may research grief and find good resources to cope with "normal" stages. But keep in mind that these are assuming the person you have lost was a decent human being.

There are additional things that accompany the loss of a relationship with an abuser, and many people do not understand the complexity of your grief and that you can't just "move on" the same as you can from a normal relationship:

- Grief often includes the discovery of a web of lies on multiple levels.
- Coming to grips with the understanding you were only being used to serve the abusers self-serving agenda.
- When you hear about him in a new relationship, it brings anxiety about what the new woman/children will endure.
- Wondering if all that time with the abuser was a complete loss in your life.
- Wondering if he will reappear in your life and what chaos and destruction will result.
- Realizing that most people just don't understand how anyone could do the things you claim he did, which reinforces a sense of isolation and alienation.

Closure, new self-awareness and strength is coming to you. You are not alone, and this part of your life has not been a waste. God can redeem and restore all you feel has been wasted and lost. Romans 8:28 says, *"We know that all things work together for good for those who love God, who are called according to his purpose."* Hold on to this promise through what seems pointless and painful.

Forgiveness

What does forgiveness mean? Does forgiveness mean I forget about everything that has happened with my abuser? Does it mean I have to stay with him or reconcile? Why can't I forgive and FEEL like I have? Does my lingering anger mean I haven't forgiven him?

Abuse victims are harangued about forgiving their abuser. These same people grant forgiveness and sympathy to the abuser, but withhold it from the victim. Churches are insidious in their favor of whoever appears to be the most believable and likable (usually the perpetrator), while judging the victim who is barely surviving. This just adds more confusion and oppression to victims, the opposite of what Christ wants.

For a long time, after we left Brian, I could not forgive him and feel it inside. I would still feel angry. I wanted to forgive and forget, and to have peace. I wanted to move on with my life without constantly remembering him. However, thoughts about him would always come again, and my negative feelings would build up like a pressure cooker.

It took time to learn about the truth of forgiveness. There's no getting around that forgiveness is commanded in Scripture. Our eternal destiny depends on it: Matthew 6:14-15, *"For if you forgive others their trespasses, your heavenly Father will also forgive you; but if you do not forgive others, neither will your Father forgive your trespasses."*

Two things I learned that helped me gain victory in this area are:

1. Forgiveness is an act of the will.

I learned to CHOOSE forgiveness. I chose forgiveness because God required it for MY well-being. If God requires something of us, then He will do the work inside us to accomplish what He wants if we are willing. God knows we are weak, and often we cannot obey Him in our own power. That's why forgiveness is an act of faith.

As I came to understand that God was not asking me to feel anything, but rather to align myself with His will, it became much easier to forgive. I stopped beating myself up for what I thought was my failure, and accepted that in the imperfection of my choice, it was all God asked of me.

Often I said through gritted teeth with tears of rage rolling down my cheeks, "God, I CHOOSE to forgive Brian. But I have no feelings of peace and release to go with it. Honor my choice to obey You and somehow cause my feelings to line up with my choice."

I did this over many months. I felt nothing different but pushed through and moved on with life until the next episode. But feelings are deceptive. One day I was out walking and enjoying a sunny peaceful day. As I walked and reflected on life, I realized, *Wow! I don't feel the anger toward Brian that I used to. In fact, I haven't even been thinking about him much!* I wasn't even sure when the last time was I had felt anything for him.

The sudden surprised recognition of peace in my heart toward Brian resulted from months, perhaps years, of God healing me inside. Each time I chose forgiveness and asked God to work it out inside me, He did — as a process I wasn't even aware of. Today I feel nothing toward Brian. I no longer have any feelings of anger I have to deal with. I have no fear, bitterness or regret. I have complete peace toward him and what happened.

2. The best kind of justice is God's justice.

Sometimes we have to let go of our right to exact revenge for abuse and injustice, and have faith in God that He will do what He says He will: Romans 12:19, *"Beloved, never avenge yourselves, but leave room for the wrath of God; for it is written, 'Vengeance is mine, I will repay,' says the Lord."*

As part of my healing process, I consoled myself that God would do that—take vengeance on Brian. I accepted that I couldn't do it, but was impatient for God to! I know full well how delightful it would be to help God along with that vengeance part! But it is not our place my friend. The Jewish Talmud offers the best advice: "Live well. It is the greatest revenge."

In time, I discovered that healing had not only produced peace toward Brian, but I had also lost the need for God's vengeance on him. Brian lost any place in my mind and heart. I know that God will deal with him — he is not my problem or concern any longer.

When you can reach this place of healing, you know you are FREE. Allow yourself to travel this path with God no matter how long it takes. God wants you to be at peace and to experience true freedom — the kind that only He can give. You were not made to carry the burden of the world's injustices on your shoulders. It is not your burden to figure out how and why each person should be punished.

Jesus says in Matthew 11:28-30, *"Come to me, all you that are weary and are carrying heavy burdens, and I will give you rest. Take my yoke upon you and learn from me; for I am gentle and humble in heart, and you will find rest for your souls. For my yoke is easy, and my burden is light."*

Let no one beat you up over the forgiveness issue. Just be willing for God to work it out inside you. He will do it in His time and way, and someday you will realize that your abuser no longer has a grip on you. When we are weak, God is strong. He is made perfect in our weakness.

Every time negative emotions and thoughts toward your (ex) husband threaten to overwhelm you, give them to God by faith. Not only will God work out peace in you, He will bring you joy. The joy of the Lord is your strength! I don't know how He works this out in us, but I know He does.

> *"but He said to me, 'My grace is sufficient for you, for power is made perfect in weakness.' So, I will boast all the more gladly of my weaknesses, so that the power of Christ may dwell in me. Therefore I am content with weaknesses, insults, hardships, persecutions and calamities for the sake of Christ; for whenever I am weak, then I am strong."*
>
> 2 Corinthians 12:9-10

Reverend Marie Fortune shares on forgiveness of abusers in her book *Keeping the Faith: Questions and Answers for the Abused Woman*:

"Take heed to yourselves; if your brother sins, rebuke him, if he repents, forgive him; and if he sins against you seven times in the day, and turns to you seven times, and says, "I repent", you must forgive him." (Luke 17:1-4)

First, Jesus says to take care of yourself. If someone abuses you (sins), rebuke him. In other words, somehow the abuser needs to hear that his behavior is wrong. This does not mean that you do it alone. It more likely means that you ask others to help you in that, perhaps the police or the pastor or other family members.

Then, Jesus says, if he repents, forgive him. This is a big if. Repentance here means more than remorse. Remorse usually gets expressed during the "making up" period of the battering cycle. The remorse may even be very genuine, but it does not mean that he will not hit again. Repentance is much more significant.

To repent, in both the Old and New Testaments, means to turn away from, to change, never to repeat again. True repentance on the part of the abuser means that he never hits again and that he learns to relate to you and/or other people in ways that are not controlling, demanding and dominating.

Forgiveness does not mean "forgiving and forgetting", implying that everything is fine now, pardoning the abuse or ignoring it. Forgiveness means putting that experience in perspective, putting it behind you and not allowing it to continue to victimize you. You can let go of it; you can remember it only when you need to. Forgiveness is for you, not for the abuser. His repentance, not your forgiveness, is what will finally bring about his healing. (57)

In the next chapter, we will look at how to overcome the giant of fear in our lives and how to experience a renewed loving relationship with God.

Reflection: Forgiveness

Forgiveness. It's imperative to move on with life and enjoy it. However, in an abusive relationship, forgiveness can seem more like pardoning, condoning, forgetting or reconciling with our abuser. We may also feel like we have to have an apology first, or explain to the person how they hurt us. None of that is necessary, and in an abusive relationship it will backfire.

Forgiveness is a choice, and it means intentionally moving toward not having constant feelings of anger toward someone for an offense, flaw, or a mistake. But first let's look at what happens if we don't forgive.

Withholding forgiveness:

- Robs us of energy we could use creatively elsewhere
- Promotes anger, depression, self-pity, distraction, suppression
- Fosters an environment of stress in both mind and body and hinders quality sleep
- Keeps us connected to that person and anchored to the past
- Creates an emotional roller coaster
- Steals joy and takes away from good relationships
- Creates a desire for medication or other unhealthy self-soothing and coping mechanisms

These consequences are not healthy, and over the long-term, they will cause more pain and long-lasting consequences than the original offense. You cannot punish someone who has done you wrong by your own feelings of anger and resentment. The only person you hurt is you.

Practicing forgiveness reduces stress and increases happiness levels. Forgiveness brings fresh perspectives and increases creativity. It opens the door for new relationships and gives the space needed to grow and thrive..

So if forgiveness is such a good thing why is it so hard to do? Why else would we refuse to forgive?

- Holding out for vindication
- Waiting for an apology that may never come
- Righteous anger
- To punish

Forgiveness is an option when you are ready, and will release you from being held hostage to that person. For a few minutes, think about these questions and see if the benefits of forgiveness outweigh the pain of holding on:

- What would it look like if you were to let go rather than hold on to this (situation, person, belief)?
- What is your underlying belief around this situation?
- Do you want to let go of this belief?
- If you could change one thing. what would it be?
- Would it be helpful to hold on to this issue for a while longer, to just let it be and let it have its space?
- How would it serve you not to change anything about this situation?
- What are the things you can control?
- What are things you cannot control?
- How does keeping this belief serve you?
- Can anything be done to change what happened?

Tips for Moving On

- Realize and acknowledge what you are doing—holding onto anger, hurt, resentment, bitterness.
- Talk to someone you can trust about your negative feelings. Let them know how you feel and why. If you don't have access to someone you can talk to, take time to talk to God about it.
- Write the pros and cons. What will happen if you let go? If you don't, what will happen? What are you willing to accept in your life? Are there things you won't accept?

- Try to understand why the person acted the way they did. With Brian, I knew why he was such a jerk. He was raised in a drug infested abusive atmosphere. Acknowledging that didn't let him off the hook because lots of people are raised in hellish circumstances and don't grow up to abuse anyone. But having that perspective still helped me see that his behavior was more about him rather than me.

- Be willing to let go.

- Forgive. This may be as simple as saying, "I forgive you." Or a ritual may be more helpful. I liked to write my grievances and then burn it up while seeing myself released from them. I have also drawn a line and then stepped over it to signify I was done with that person sabotaging any more of my life. Pick something meaningful to you.

- Use this as an opportunity to grow. By showing yourself the compassion you deserve, you can change your life. How exciting is that? Jump-start your transformation by learning from your mistakes. Always seek opportunities for growth.

- Identify one person who you need to forgive and start the process above. It doesn't have to be the hardest one; you can start with the easiest and build your forgiveness "muscle." Maybe you blame yourself and it's time to forgive yourself with compassion and kindness.

- Go at your own pace, be patient, and be gentle with yourself. This process may need to be done many times. But if you are determined to be free, you will see the tentacles on your heart and mind lose their grip one by one.

"We can't control what others do that hurt us. We can only control what we do in response to that hurt."

Foundation

"Lord, you are so good to me, so kind in every way and ready to forgive, for your grace-fountain keeps overflowing, drenching all your lovers who pray to you."

Psalm 86:5 (TPT)

"Everything Has Its Time, For everything there is a season, and a time for every matter under heaven:

a time to be born, and a time to die;
a time to plant, and a time to pluck up what is planted;
a time to kill, and a time to heal;
a time to break down, and a time to build up;
a time to weep, and a time to laugh;
a time to mourn, and a time to dance;
a time to throw away stones, and a time to gather stones together;
a time to embrace, and a time to refrain from embracing;
a time to seek, and a time to lose;
a time to keep, and a time to throw away;
a time to tear, and a time to sew;
a time to keep silence, and a time to speak;
a time to love, and a time to hate;
a time for war, and a time for peace."

Ecclesiastes 3:1-8

"Do not fret because of the wicked; do not be envious of wrongdoers, for they will soon fade like the grass, and wither like the green herb. Trust in the Lord, and do good; so you will live in the land, and enjoy security. Take delight in the Lord, and He will give you the desires of your heart.

Commit your way to the Lord; trust in Him, and He will act. He will make your vindication shine like the light, and the justice of your cause like the noonday."

Psalm 37:1-6

Chapter 16

Freedom from Fear

THE PREDOMINANT UNDERLYING issue I battled through the years was fear. Even before I married Brian, I felt afraid of many things. Fear has a way of either paralyzing us so we are indecisive when we need to take action, or pressuring us so we decide quickly (which is normally unwise). Perhaps you can identify with some of what I felt:

Fear of…

- being alone caused me to jump recklessly into my marriage with Brian, ignoring all the red flags of a future abusive relationship.
- disappointing God caused me to submit to things I should never have submitted to.
- Brian caused me to stay quiet and not stand up to him.
- the future caused me to think I would never have it any better anyway.
- losing my children caused me to decide not to do anything to fight the abuse.

- unemployment, homelessness and not being able to provide for my children caused me to stay with Brian.
- being alone again.
- Brian's revenge if I stood up to him or left.
- Brian hurting the children.
- if I tried to hide, he would find me.
- reaching out to others for any help or friendship because Brian might hurt them.
- rejection and not being believed if I spoke up.

Fear produces other feelings such as helplessness, hopelessness, despair, depression, confusion and many more. Many of these fears are also contradictory which just increases paralysis. Once fear gets a grip, it doesn't let go easily.

The list I gave has one common thread through it. Everything is the opposite of God's way of doing and being. So if it is not of God, and it is not an instinct to imminent danger, then the other source is the flesh or the demonic realm. It is important to learn about and confront a favorite tool of the enemy to keep us out of God's will.

"*Fear not!*" is the most repeated command in the Bible. God knows Satan uses fear to overcome us, and He commands us to take an active role in resisting it. To be free of fear, we must eliminate the habits of fear-based thinking and relating with God and others. We have to learn to rely on the truth of God's Word.

There are two types of fear beyond the God-given instinct to flee danger: fear of God and a spirit of fear. Did you know humans worship what they fear? Fear is an act of worship! In both the Hebrew and Greek, there are two words for worship.

The first kind means to bow down, to kneel, and to put one's face down as an act of respect and submission. The attitude of the heart is saying, "I will obey whatever you command of me." The other word means to serve. Half of the time these words are translated as worship, and the other half as serve. They carry the idea of making a sacrifice or carrying out instructions.

Worship involves three acts: speaking, listening, doing. Worship involves the mind and heart and doing something. Think of this in connection with living with our abusers. Are we worshiping our abuser, and the one working through him (not God!) Or, are we worshiping the Lord God?

Fear of God

Fear of God is a good thing and means respect and reverence of Him because He is Creator, Master, Judge, King… and we are not. God alone is supreme and no one can stand against His decrees. The cosmos itself bows to Him. However, God is not a cruel dictator ready to lower the boom when we slip up. Instead, He is kind and patient with us. Fearing God holds many blessings and benefits such as wisdom, understanding, life, peace, contentment, joy, safety and security. (Psalm 111:10; Proverbs 1:7, 14:26-27, 19:23)

> *"The [reverent] fear of the Lord [that is, worshiping Him and regarding Him as truly awesome] is the beginning and the preeminent part of wisdom [its starting point and its essence], And the knowledge of the Holy One is understanding and spiritual insight."*
>
> Proverbs 9:10 (AMP)

Spirit of Fear

The second type of fear is a "spirit of fear." A spirit of fear brings destruction, torment and bondage and is from the kingdom of darkness.

> *"For God did not give us a spirit of timidity or cowardice or fear, but [He has given us a spirit] of power and of love and of sound judgment and personal discipline [abilities that result in a calm, well-balanced mind and self-control]."*
>
> 2 Timothy 1:7 (AMP)

Whoever we set our thoughts upon the most, our heart's desire, our fear, our servitude—whoever sits on the throne of our heart is the one we are worshiping. When we need a miracle, we need to worship God.

When I woke up after sleeping on the beach in Chile, and went for a walk to talk to God and plead with Him for help out of our desperate situation, He gave me a revelation of this. I wanted His help and blessing, but He was second place to Brian, and that was not okay with Him. I hadn't even realized over the years how Brian had usurped God's position on the throne of my heart. But he had.

Before marrying Brian, even though I had hang-ups and made mistakes, God was first place in my heart and mind. I loved God so much, thought about Him often, talked to Him, and listened to Him. I felt so in love with Him and loved back. All I wanted to do was please Him. As long as I maintained this relationship, it seemed like life went smoothly and I enjoyed the blessings that come with an intimate relationship with God.

I also had a healthy respect for Him. Our friendship did not minimize He was God of the universe and I was not. In fact, the closer I felt to Him, the more I recognized His holiness and my need for Him as my Savior. There was no spirit of fear attached to it. The closer I walked with God, the less fear I felt, and the fewer mistakes I made in life.

> *"There is no fear in love [dread does not exist]. But perfect (complete, full-grown) love drives out fear, because fear involves [the expectation of divine] punishment, so the one who is afraid [of God's judgment] is not perfected in love [has not grown into a sufficient understanding of God's love]."*
>
> 1 John 4:18 (AMP)

When I slid backwards in my relationship with Him, fear was at the door ready to step in and take up residence. When I met Brian, I ignored my God-given instincts warning me of danger. I justified Brian as God's will for my life. However, I did that because I was in a personal crisis and afraid of being alone. Rather than turning to God for peace and wisdom, I plunged forward driven by fear. The enemy had someone ready to step in and take me down a destructive path.

When I married Brian, I still thought God was first place. In fact, Brian was very insistent that God be first place in our marriage and lives. But oh how deceptive and twisted the enemy of our souls can be! Fear does this. It warps our reasoning and ability to see truth.

The reality was that Brian was serving a master other than God, no matter how much he proclaimed otherwise. Brian gradually replaced God in my mind, heart and actions. I thought about Brian all the time — how could I please him, how could I be in his favor, what could I do for him, what did he want from me, and on and on. Only this "worship" produced the fruit of unrighteousness — fear, torment, compromised values and constant worry. A spirit of fear had taken charge, and it was a harsh taskmaster.

The morning on the beach in Chile, God showed me He needed to be back on the throne of my heart. I needed to get my values straight before the rest of my miserable life could be repaired. Once I saw the truth of this, I gladly repented to Him for my failure to worship and serve Him alone.

I accepted that I had made choices that were driven by fear rather than faith. I couldn't blame Brian for all of it. Even though I thought my passivity was justified, I realized that I had a free will and if I had faith in God, I never had to accept the treatment I received.

God calls His children to abide in truth and righteousness, never passive and accepting of whatever comes along. Passivity is from Satan to keep us in bondage so we don't fulfill God's plan for our lives. There is a big difference between waiting because God is asking us to, and we have His peace; and being passive because fear paralyzes us.

God wanted me to put Him first again and be filled with peace and trust in Him. When I repented and put God back on the throne of my heart, I didn't have a clue how anything would work out, but I had a deep sense of peace I hadn't had in a long time. Fear was still there, trying to take back its seat of imminence, but I clung to God and resisted it the best I could. God honored my obedience and faith and rescued us miraculously.

Overcoming fear in our lives is a process, and it doesn't mean fear ever stops trying to gain a foothold. The more entrenched fear is, the more we may need support from other believers to help us gain victory. Look at the difference in the next two verses:

"When I am afraid, I will put my trust and faith in You."

Psalm 56:3 (AMP)

> *"Behold, God, my salvation! I will trust and not be afraid, For the Lord God is my strength and song; Yes, He has become my salvation."*
>
> Isaiah 12:2 (AMP)

The first writer acknowledges fear has already taken hold, but resists and trusts in the Lord. In the second one, the writer's faith has matured to where trust is dominant and fear does not even gain an entry. Our faith in Jesus grows, matures, and keeps us from fear.

> *"The Lord is my light and my salvation; whom shall I fear? The Lord is the stronghold of my life; of whom shall I be afraid?"*
>
> Psalm 27:1

Turning on our faith is like turning on a light in a dark room. When we walk into a dark room, we do not shoo out the darkness or fight it with our fists. We turn on the light and the darkness flees. Faith is the light switch that causes the darkness of fear to flee. We get faith by being filled with the Word of God and proclaiming its truths over our lives: Romans 10:17, *"So faith comes from what is heard, and what is heard comes through the word of Christ."* James 4:7, *"Submit yourselves therefore to God. Resist the devil, and he will flee from you."*

It is important to realize that the devil has certain power. He wields most of his power through fear. However, Jesus calls him a liar when He speaks to the hypocritical religious leaders in John 8:44 (AMP), *"You are of your father the devil, and it is your will to practice the desires [which are characteristic] of your father. He was a murderer from the beginning, and does not stand in the truth because there is no truth in him. When he lies, he speaks what it natural to him, for he is a liar and the father of lies and half-truths."*

The power of God is much greater than the power of Satan. It is much greater than the power of those who serve the kingdom of darkness, such as abusive people. The way they act and talk it can seem like they are powerful, but their power pales in comparison to the Lord's.

> *"Little children (believers, dear ones), you are of God and you belong to Him and have [already] overcome them [the agents of the antichrist]; because He who is in you is greater than he (Satan) who is in the world [of sinful mankind]."*
>
> 1 John 4:4 (AMP)

All of hell and Satan himself is subject to the power of Jesus. Matthew 28:18, *"And Jesus came and said to them, All authority in heaven and on earth has been given to me."*

You are not stronger than the devil, but Jesus is. When fear and worry attacks you, you can pray in the name of Jesus, resist and overcome it.

> *"Listen carefully: I have given you authority [that you now possess] to tread on serpents and scorpions, and [the ability to exercise authority] over all the power of the enemy (Satan); and nothing will [in any way] harm you."*
>
> Luke 10:19 (AMP)

This authority is yours if you belong to Him, believe His Word and pray in His name. The Bible speaks of the power of coming into agreement with other believers.

> *"How could one have routed a thousand, and two put a myriad to flight, unless their Rock had sold them, the Lord had given them up?"*
>
> Matthew 18:19 (AMP)

> *"Again I say to you, that if two believers on earth agree [that is, are of one mind, in harmony] about anything that they ask [within the will of God], it will be done for them by My Father in heaven."*
>
> Deuteronomy 32:30

If you do not pray Scripture, you may like to start by using what I pray over myself and my family. I compiled some of them in Appendix G. Personalize them to fit your life. You may go through legal battles and have to deal with different agencies. Perhaps you are in hiding, or still live with your abuser. No matter what obstacle you are facing, no matter what your greatest fear is, God is bigger: *"For nothing will be impossible with God."* (Luke 1:37)

What is important is to build and maintain a relationship with God through praying His Word over yourself and your family. The more you meditate on and pray God's Word, faith will get bigger and fear and torment will lose its grip on you. Ask God to give you a promise from His Word to sustain you. He will do it! Then hold on to it and believe it.

Whenever fear and doubt come to your mind, speak out the Word to counteract it. This is showing who your faith is in and who you are choosing to worship. Put God first place every day and resist what Satan brings against you. You will see situations turn around that seemed impossible. Things might not go exactly the way you think they should, but God in His wisdom will work all things for good. You will see that in hindsight. Trust in God is never misplaced.

Reflection: Fear

Fear. It keeps us stuck and "safe" in our comfort zone, holding us back from engaging with life the way we wish we could. In toxic or abusive relationships, we seek or create a sense of safety from that which we fear. However, there is no real safety because safety requires someone or something we must be safe from.

Fear is hard-wired into us to keep us protected from perceived threats, but it also protects us from growth and good change. When we face our fear rather than pushing it away or trying to get rid of it, we can move forward. These questions will help you identify your fear and move past it.

- What are you afraid of?
- Is this fear real or imagined? How do you know?
- What would you do if you knew you couldn't fail?
- If you do not take action toward what you want, what will things be like?
- If you take action, how will things change?
- Why is it important to you to have what you want?
- What small step could you take towards your goal that feels safe?
- What is your next step?

Tips to Shift from Fear to Freedom

- Identify and deal with hidden ways fear is showing up and holding you back. See the worksheet on gremlins for easy tactics to do this.
- Challenge your fear with facts. Find evidence to the contrary and reject your fear-fed limitations.
- If your fear is valid, take practical action to mitigate potential problems.
- Let go of the need for approval from others, but get the support of those who care about you and can offer wisdom.
- Be compassionate with yourself. You are always learning and growing. Even the hard times can be full of good things and beauty. If you fall short, it's not the end of the world. Keep moving forward anyway!
- Instead of repeating "I can't," change it to "I can…"
- Look for deeper meaning and ask, "What do I need to learn from this?"

Foundation

"For God did not give us a spirit of timidity or cowardice or fear, but [He has given us a spirit] of power and of love and of sound judgment and personal discipline [abilities that result in a calm, well-balanced mind and self-control]."

2 Timothy 1:7 (AMP)

"There is no fear in love, but perfect love casts out fear; for fear has to do with punishment, and whoever fears has not reached perfection in love."

1 John 4:18

"Let your character [your moral essence, your inner nature] be free from the love of money [shun greed—be financially ethical], being content with what you have; for He has said, "I will never [under any circumstances] desert you [nor give you up nor leave you without support, nor will I in any degree leave you helpless], nor will I forsake or let you down or relax My hold on you [assuredly not]!" So we take comfort and are encouraged and confidently say, 'The Lord is my Helper [in time of need], I will not be afraid. What will man do to me?'"

Hebrews 13:5-6 (AMP)

Thank you for spending time with me in the pages of this book. I hope that something here has touched your heart and given hope and inspiration to you to continue to move forward. Do not give up! One day the trials you are enduring really will end. Perhaps you will find ways, as I have, to come alongside others and help them through their pain. We need each other for strength and encouragement. In the hands of God, your life is not over, your purpose is not extinguished, your past is not wasted, and your children are not lost. I pray for God's blessings on you and your children, His peace to envelope you, and His joy to strengthen you!

> *"Press Onward! We all make mistakes. It's time we stop dwelling on them and move forward. Ask for forgiveness from others, forgive yourself and then…full steam ahead. Darkness has no greater companion than a self loathing unforgiven or unforgiving heart. Paul writes in Philippians: "…But one thing I do, forgetting what is behind and straining toward what is ahead, I press on toward the goal…" Press on dear friends for life, love and joy await you!"*
>
> ~ Jason Versey

Appendix A

Chronic Personality Problems

Condensed from article on *Psychology Today* by Sandra L. Brown M.A. https://www.psychologytoday.com/us/blog/pathological-relationships/200912/chronic-personality-problems-in-problem-relationships)

A large portion of abusers (although not all) have some similar identifying disorders, traits or diagnosis. They are not all created equal. That means each one of them brings a unique combination of traits, challenges and problems to the equation of the relationship and even therapy.

Therefore, not all abusers treatment is going to be effective because not all psychological problems are treatable... Some of the disorders have biological and neurological root causes that are not curable. Ultimately, not all problem relationships have a solution, especially those that have biological and neuro problems at their basis.

Related to Antisocial Personality Disorder:
- Disregard for, and the violation of, the rights of others
- Failure to conform to lawful social norms

- Deceitfulness, impulsivity or failure to plan ahead
- Irritability and aggressiveness as indicated by repeated physical fights or assaults
- Reckless disregard for the safety of self or others
- Consistent irresponsibility as indicated by repeated failure to sustain consistent work behavior or honor financial obligations

Related to Sociopaths and Psychopaths:
- Lack of remorse as indicated by being indifferent about having hurt, mistreated or stolen from another
- Glib and superficial charm
- Grandiose (exaggeratedly high) estimation of self
- Need for stimulation
- Pathological lying
- Cunning and manipulativeness
- Lack of remorse or guilt
- Shallow affect (superficial emotional responsiveness)
- Callousness and lack of empathy
- Parasitic lifestyle
- Poor behavioral controls
- Sexual promiscuity
- Early behavior problems
- Lack of realistic long-term goals
- Impulsivity, irresponsibility
- Failure to accept responsibility for own actions
- Many short-term relationships

- Juvenile delinquency
- Revocation of conditional release
- Criminal versatility

Related to Borderline Personality Disorder:

- Frantic efforts to avoid real or imagined abandonment
- Intense and unstable personal relationships that over idealize and devalue
- Identity disturbance with unstable self-image or sense of self impulsivity in at least two areas (spending, sex, substance abuse, reckless driving, binge eating)
- Recurrent suicidal behavior, gestures, threats or self-mutilation
- Emotional instability due to a marked reactivity of mood (intense episodic irritability or anxiety)
- Chronic feelings of emptiness
- Inappropriate intense anger or difficulty controlling anger

Related to Narcissistic Personality Disorder:

- A grandiose sense of self importance
- Exaggerates their achievements and talents
- Expects to be recognized as superior without commensurate achievements
- Is preoccupied with fantasies of unlimited success, power, brilliance, beauty, or ideal love
- Believes that he is special and unique and can only be understood by, or should only associate with, other special or other high-status people or institutions
- Requires excessive admiration

- Has a sense of entitlement, unreasonable expectations of especially favorable treatment or automatic compliance with his expectations
- In interpersonally exploitative within relationships and takes advantage of others to achieve his own ends
- Lacks empathy and is unwilling to recognize or identify with the feelings and needs of others
- Is often envious of others or believes that others are envious of him
- Shows an arrogant, haughty behavior or attitude

This list is not mild relational infractions… The permanent forms of pathology are noted for its *Three Inabilities* (Brown, 2005):

1. Inability to grow to any authentic emotional or spiritual depth
2. Inability to sustain positive change
3. Inability to develop insight how their behavior negatively affects others

These inabilities are the hallmark of chronic disorders that create chronic problem relationships. (More info at www.saferelationships-magazine.com)

Appendix B
21 Signs of an Abusive Parent

(Condensed from full article at https://themighty.com/2018/09/abusive-parent-signs/)

In an abusive relationship, the children suffer the most. If we were raised in a dysfunctional home, we might be unintentionally hurting our children, not realizing our behavior is toxic or even abusive. These signs will hopefully lead to changes for the emotional safety and well-being of your precious kids. Please put them first and get them counseling and support. Your local women's shelter or crisis center should have kids resources to share with you. The full article by Juliette Virzi is a must read.

Here are some "signs" of an abusive parent we need to talk about:

1. Withholding or Making a Child "Earn" Basic Necessities

    Parents who maliciously deprive their children of their basic needs or make their children feel guilty for receiving the things a parent is obligated to provide are abusive.

2. "Parentification" or Enmeshment

    … boundaries are blurred and the child can end up feeling less like a child and more like a romantic partner.

3. Favoring One Child Over Another

    … favorite children can grow up with a distorted, inflated view of themselves, while unfavored children can grow up with a distorted, negative view of themselves.

4. Incessant Teasing/Humiliation

    … a classic sign of childhood emotional abuse is the use of shame and humiliation. This can include harsh, incessant teasing or putting a child down in front of an audience.

5. Not Giving a Child Privacy

    Not allowing a child to have age-appropriate privacy may impact their ability to trust others, maintain their own boundaries and respect the boundaries of others.

6. Threatening Physical Violence (Even If There Is No Intent to Actually Use Violence)

    Even if no physical harm is actually done, this kind of fear tactic is emotionally abusive, and may be just as damaging as actual physical abuse.

7. Making Siblings "Compete" for Love and Approval

    … actively encouraging and "pitting" siblings against each other. It reinforces the lie that parental love should be "earned" instead of freely and unconditionally given.

8. Using Religion to Shame a Child

    Using religion to shame a child (as opposed to lovingly pointing them to spiritual values) can be damaging because in many religions, God is a father figure.

9. Emotional Neglect or Being Absent

    Sometimes abusive behavior is less about what a parent *does* to a child and more about what they *don't* do. This can be incredibly damaging to a child because they … often struggling with their mental health and self-esteem as a result.

10. Showing Love Conditionally

    When parents give love conditionally, children ... may struggle with perfectionism and trying to "earn" love.

11. Using a Child to "Get Back" at the Other Parent

    Putting a child in the middle of an argument between parents is emotionally abusive.

12. Accepting Nothing Short of Perfection

    Expecting perfection from a child can teach children they will only be loved if they perform well ... can make children excessively self-critical and undermine their confidence and self-belief.

13. Constant "Guilt-Tripping"

    Being "guilt-tripped" by an authority figure like a parent can cause real damage, often making it hard for a child to assert healthy boundaries in adulthood.

14. Playing the Victim and Always Blaming the Child

    This kind of behavior is emotionally abusive because it models a failure to take ownership for wrongdoing.

15. Never Allowing a Child to Communicate His/Her Own Needs

    Curbing a child's ability to speak for him or herself when he/she is able can be abusive. Children should be made to feel safe expressing their needs and emotions...

16. Verbal Abuse or Ridicule as "Discipline"

    In a study examining whether childhood verbal abuse increased the risk for developing personality disorders (PDs), it was found that childhood verbal abuse may contribute to development of some kinds of PDs and other co-occuring psychiatric disorders.

17. Telling a Child to "Stop Crying" or Calling Them "Too Sensitive"

    A vital part of growing up is developing a separate identity from your parent, particularly when it comes to expressing emotions.

18. Violating a Child's Age-Appropriate Boundaries, Saying It's a Parental "Right"

    Not allowing a child to assert his/her own boundaries on the grounds of parental "right" can be abusive.

19. Constantly Invalidating a Child's Struggles

    Invalidation is a prime example of emotional abuse—especially when it's used to justify poor parenting practices on the basis of "it could have been worse."

20. Stealing or Taking the Money a Child Earned

    Parents who feel entitled to the money their children makes because they supported and provided for their children can act abusively.

21. Making Your Child Who You Want Them to Be vs. Who They Want to Be

    In an effort to see children "realize their potential," some parents try to mold their children into who they think they should be ... potentially leading to poor self-esteem and perfectionism.

Appendix C

Risk Assessment

There is a free MOSAIC threat assessment here: https://www.mosaicmethod.com/. The MOSAIC method works by breaking a situation down to its elements and then seeing what picture emerges when the pieces of the puzzle are put together.

Another excellent tool is available here: https://www.dangerassessment.org/DATools.aspx

Abusive relationships often become more violent over time. While it is impossible to predict with any degree of certainty when relationships will escalate to lethal violence, researchers have identified some common factors. Lack of the following circumstances does not necessarily indicate that violence will not become lethal. Abused women should always use extreme care in planning for safety and should rely on their own instincts in determining appropriate responses to violent situations. Although lethality assessments can be useful, you are the best judge of the danger your batterer poses to you and your children.

Lundy Bancroft offers the following factors that should be taken particularly seriously. The full article is on his webpage at:

http://lundybancroft.com/articles/assessing-dangerousness-in-men-who-abuse-women/

- The woman has a strong "gut" sense that the man could kill her or her children, or could carry out a serious and dangerous assault against any of them or against himself.

- He is extremely jealous and possessive. This characteristic becomes even more worrisome when he appears to be obsessive, constantly keeping her at the center of his thoughts and appearing to be unable to conceive of life without her. He has, for example, made statements such as, "If I can't have you, nobody will."

- He has a history of severe or very frequent violence toward her, or toward other individuals such as past partners.

- He follows her, monitors her whereabouts, uses high-tech means to keep tabs on her, or stalks her in other ways. He knows where she lives and works, knows names and addresses of her friend or relatives, or is in very familiar with her daily routines.

- She is taking steps to end the relationship, or has already done so.

- He was violent to her during a pregnancy.

- There are stepchildren involved.

- He has threatened to kill her or to hurt her severely, has strangled her, or has threatened her with a weapon (including making verbal reference to using a weapon, even if he did not actually brandish it).

- He has threatened to kill the children or the whole family.

- He has access to weapons and/or he is familiar with their use.

- He is depressed, suicidal, or shows signs of not caring what happens to him. He has, for example, threatened to kill himself if she leaves him.
- He is unemployed.
- He isn't close to anyone, and no current relationships with friends or relatives are important to him.
- He has a significant criminal history and/or he has a history of using violence or threatening violence against other people.
- He abuses alcohol or drugs heavily, especially if his habits involve daily or nearly daily intoxication.
- He has been violent to children.
- He has killed or in other ways been violent to pets, or has used other terror tactics.
- He uses pornography heavily and/or has a history or perpetrating sexual violence or degradation against his partner or others.
- He has exhibited extreme behaviors when his current partner or past partners have made attempts to leave him.

Appendix D

Safety Plan

Safety planning is a crucial step. The following practical plans can help you stay safe while you are still with your abuser, as you prepare to leave, and after the relationship has ended.

IF YOU ARE STILL WITH YOUR ABUSER

- Try to avoid an abusive situation by leaving.
- Identify safe areas of the house where there are no weapons and there are ways to escape. If arguments occur, try to move to those areas.
- Don't run to where the children are, as your partner may hurt them as well.
- If violence is unavoidable, make yourself a small target; dive into a corner and curl up into a ball with your face protected and arms around each side of your head, fingers entwined.
- If possible, have a phone accessible at all times and know what numbers to call for help. Know where the nearest pay phone is located. Know the phone number to your local shelter (RDAP's crisis hotline is available 24 hours a day at 308-534-3495). Don't be afraid to call the police.

- Let trusted friends and neighbors know of your situation and develop a plan and visual signal for when you need help.
- Practice how to get out safely. Practice with your children.
- Teach your children how to get help. Instruct them not to get involved in the violence between you and your partner. Plan a code word to signal to them that they should get help or leave the house.
- Tell your children that violence is never right, even when someone they love is being violent. Tell them that neither you, nor they, are at fault or are the cause of the violence, and that when anyone is being violent, it is important to stay safe.
- Keep weapons like guns and knives locked away and as inaccessible as possible.
- Make a habit of backing the car into the driveway and keeping it fueled. Keep the driver's door unlocked and others locked—for a quick escape.
- Create several plausible reasons for leaving the house at different times of the day or night.
- Call a domestic violence hotline periodically to assess your options and get a supportive understanding ear.

PREPARING TO LEAVE YOUR ABUSER

- Keep any evidence of physical abuse, such as pictures.
- Know where you can go to get help; tell someone what is happening to you.
- If you are injured, go to a doctor or an emergency room and report what happened to you. Ask that they document your visit.
- Plan for what you will do if your children tell your partner

of your plan or if your partner otherwise finds out about your plan.

- Plan with your children and identify a safe place for them, like a room with a lock or a friend's house where they can go for help. Reassure them that their job is to stay safe, not to protect you.
- Contact RDAP or your local crisis center to find out about laws and other resources available to you before you have to use them during a crisis.
- Keep a journal of all violent incidences, noting dates, events and threats made, if possible.
- Acquire job skills or take courses at a community college as you can.
- Try to set money aside or ask friends or family members to hold money for you.

If you need to sneak away, be prepared:

- Make a plan for how and where you will escape. Don't be afraid to request a police stand-by or escort while you leave.
- Plan for a quick escape.
- Put aside emergency money as you can.
- Hide an extra set of car keys.
- Pack an extra set of clothes for yourself and your children and store them at a trusted friend or neighbor's house. Try to avoid using the homes of next-door neighbors, close family members and mutual friends.

Take with you important phone numbers of friends, relatives, doctors, schools, etc., as well as other important items, including:

- Driver's license
- Regularly needed medication

- Credit cards or a list of credit cards you hold yourself or jointly
- Pay stubs
- Checkbooks and information about bank accounts and other assets

If time is available, also take:
- Citizenship documents (such as your passport, green card, etc.)
- Titles, deeds and other property information
- Medical records
- Children's school and immunization records
- Insurance information
- Copy of marriage license, birth certificates, will and other legal documents
- Verification of social security numbers
- Welfare identification
- Valued pictures, jewelry or personal possessions

AFTER YOU LEAVE YOUR ABUSER

If the offender is leaving your home:
- Change your locks and phone number.
- Change your work hours and usual route to and from work.
- Change the route taken to transport children to and from school.

If you are leaving or moving to a new residence:
- Consider renting a post office box or using the address of a friend for your mail.

- Be aware that addresses are on restraining orders and police reports.
- Be careful to whom you give your new address and phone number.
- Change your work hours, if possible.
- Alert school authorities of the situation.
- Consider changing your children's schools.

If you need to get a restraining order, RDAP (or your local dv agency) can help. After you have the order in place:

- Keep a certified copy of your restraining order with you at all times.
- Inform friends, neighbors and employers that you have a restraining order in effect.
- Give copies of the restraining order to employers, neighbors and schools along with a picture of the offender.
- Call law enforcement to enforce the order if necessary.

In general, the following measures can help you stay safe after leaving an abuser.

- Reschedule appointments that the offender is aware of.
- Use different stores and frequent different social spots.
- Alert neighbors and request that they call the police if they feel you may be in danger.
- Talk to trusted people about the violence.
- Replace wooden doors with steel or metal doors. Install security systems if possible.
- Install a motion sensitive lighting system.
- Tell people you work with about the situation and have your calls screened by one receptionist if possible.

- Tell people who take care of your children who can pick up your children. Explain your situation to them and provide them with a copy of the restraining order, if you have one.
- Call the telephone company to request caller ID for any landlines. Ask that your phone number be blocked so that if you call anyone, neither your former partner nor anyone else will be able to get your new, unlisted phone number.

This information was taken from the Rape and Domestic Abuse Program at https://nprdap.org/safety-planning/. Some information is Copyright © 1998 by the National Center for Victims of Crime. This information may be freely distributed, provided that it is distributed free of charge, in its entirety and includes this copyright notice.

Appendix E
Technology Safety Plan

Technology can be helpful to victims of domestic violence, sexual violence and stalking. However it is important to consider how technology might be misused. These condensed tips come from the *National Network to End Domestic Violence*: https://nnedv.org/ See the links below for more tips for your specific needs.

- Trust your instincts. If you suspect an abusive person knows too much, it is possible that your phone, computer, email, driving or other activities are being monitored. Abusers and stalkers can act in incredibly persistent and creative ways to maintain power and control.

- Have your car checked. If the abusive person knows where you are whenever you are in your car, you may consider having your car checked for hidden location devices. Ask a trusted mechanic or law enforcement to check the car thoroughly.

- Plan for safety. Navigating violence, abuse, and stalking is very difficult and dangerous. Contact local and provincial/territory domestic violence or rape crisis hot-lines and organizations to discuss options and safety risks. The Safety Net

Project (https://nnedv.org/content/safety-net/) can support agencies in any technology stalking or safety issues you experience that are new or unfamiliar to their staff.

- Take precautions if you have a "techy" abuser. If computers and technology are a profession or hobby for the abuser/stalker, trust your instincts. If you think someone may be monitoring or tracking you, talk to hot-line advocates or police.

- Hidden cameras. If you suspect cameras in your home, figure out where the camera is hidden based on the information shared by the abusive person or gifts to you or members of your household from the abuser. Some camera detectors may be helpful in locating the cameras, but remember that some detectors will only locate wireless cameras or wired cameras. Either remove the camera or if that may be dangerous, limit what you do in the room that is being monitored. If your computer/tablet has built-in web camera, consider disabling the camera when you aren't using it. Or you can cover the camera with a piece of removable tape.

- Use a safer computer. If anyone abusive has access to your computer, he/she might be monitoring your computer activities. Try to use a safer computer when you look for help, a new place to live, etc. It may be safer to use a computer at a public library, community center, or Internet café.

- Create new email or IM accounts. If you suspect that anyone abusive can access your email or instant messaging (IM), consider creating additional email/IM accounts on a safer computer. Do not create or check this new email/IM from a computer the abuser could access, in case it is monitored. Look for free web-based email accounts, and strongly consider using non-identifying name & account information.

(example: bluecat@email.com and not YourRealName@email.com)

- Check your cell phone settings. If you are using a cell phone provided by the abusive person, consider turning it off when not in use. Also, many phones let you "lock" the keys so a phone won't automatically answer or call if bumped. When on, check the phone settings; if your phone has an optional location service, you may want to switch the location feature off/on via phone settings or by turning your phone on and off.

- Get a new or donated cell phone. If you suspect that your cell phone is being monitored, the safest thing is to get a new phone with an account that the abusive person doesn't have access to. A pay-as-you-go phone is an inexpensive alternative. Put a pass-code on your phone and ensure that location settings and Bluetooth settings are turned off. When making or receiving private calls or arranging escape plans, try not to use a shared or family cell phone because cell phone billing records and phone logs might reveal your plans to an abuser. Contact your local or provincial/territory hot-line/crisis organization to learn about donation programs that provide new free cell phones and/or prepaid phone cards to victims of abuse and stalking.

- Change passwords & pin numbers. Some abusers use victim's email and other accounts to impersonate and cause harm. If anyone abusive knows or could guess your passwords, change them quickly and frequently. Think about any password protected accounts: online banking, voicemail, instant messaging, etc.

- Minimize use of cordless phones or baby monitors. If you don't want others to overhear your conversations, turn off baby monitors if not needed and use traditional corded phones for sensitive conversations.

- Ask about your records and data. Some court systems, government agencies and organizations publish records with personal information on the Internet. Ask agencies how they protect or publish your records and request that court, government, post office and others seal or restrict access to your files to protect your safety.

- Get a private mailbox and don't give out your real address. When asked by businesses, doctors, and others for your address, have a private mailbox address or a safer address to provide. Try to keep your true residential address out of databases. Inquire about address confidentiality programs.

- Search for your name on the Internet. Major search engines such as "Google" or "Yahoo" may have links to your contact information. Search for your name in quotation marks: "Full Name." Check phone directory pages because unlisted numbers might be listed if you gave your number to anyone.

- Limit the information you give out about yourself. Most things we do these days ask for personally identifying information – whether it is to make a purchase, open a discount card or create an account. Limit the information that you provide since you don't know who else they will share your information with.

- Document the incidences. If possible, document the stalking or harassing behavior.

- Report the incidences. If you feel safe in doing so, report the incidences to law enforcement and ask for a police report. If the harassing behavior is online, report it to the website. Many sites have links where you can report abusive content.

- "Smart" and "connected" toys that promise to entertain,

increase safety, and connect us to our kids and pets while we're away from home are rushing into the marketplace. These devices may offer survivors ways to increase privacy and safety, with knowledge about privacy settings and strategic use. Unfortunately, they can also provide yet another, highly invasive way that technology can be misused to monitor, harass, threaten, or harm survivors.

- Think about your safety. Oftentimes, many victims want to stop the abusive behavior by getting rid of the technology. However, for some abusive individuals, this may escalate their controlling and dangerous behavior if they feel their control is threatened and you are removing all access. Think about what may happen if you remove the camera or the GPS. Incorporate that into your safety planning. For example, some survivors choose to use a safer computer, device or phone, but not disabling the monitored device to continue collecting evidence.

Comprehensive Resource List for Technology Safety:

https://nnedv.org/resources/?mdocs-cat=mdocs-cat-8#

Safety tips include Technology Safety Quick Tips, Steps to Increasing Your Browser Privacy, State-by-State Listing of Address Confidentiality Programs, Spyware and Safety, Privacy and Safety Tips When Relocating, High-Tech Stalking, and more.

Hundreds of Apps Can Empower Stalkers to Track Their Victims:

https://www.nytimes.com/2018/05/19/technology/phone-apps-stalking.html?action=click&module=RelatedCoverage&pgtype=Article&region=Footer

Thermostats, Locks and Lights: Digital Tools of Domestic Abuse:

https://www.nytimes.com/2018/06/23/technology/smart-home-devices-domestic-abuse.html

Appendix F

Pet Safety and Custody

Offenders harm pets as a tactic of domestic violence – to hurt victims, to gain power and control, and to intimidate or coerce victims to stay. In many cases, perpetrators of domestic violence may kill, harm, or threaten pets in order to assert their dominance and "emotionally blackmail" victims into complying with and remaining silent about the abuse victims are experiencing. [http://nationallinkcoalition.org/wp-content/uploads/2014/06/Allies-Link-Monograph-2014.pdf]

According to the American Society for the Prevention of Cruelty to Animals (ASPCA), seventy-one percent of pet-owning women entering domestic violence shelters reported that the abuser threatened, harmed, or killed the family pet. [http://www.aspca.org/blog/protecting-all-victims-domestic-violence]

Animal abuse can also be an indicator of domestic violence and is an early warning sign of concurrent or future violence. [http://nationallinkcoalition.org/what-is-the-link]

If you are in an abusive situation and have pets, please read these tips by Allie Phillips of *Sheltering Animals and Families Together*

(SAF-T): https://alliephillips.com/wp-content/uploads/2018/10/Safety-Planning-Brochure-2018-4.jpeg?x10201

- Ask friends, family or co-workers if they can care for your pet while you seek safety at a shelter.
- Contact your local family violence shelter and ask if they will accept you and your pet.
- Ask the family violence shelter if they have a pet foster care program or can refer you to a safe pet boarding facility.
- Before leaving, create a pet bag that includes vet records, especially recent vaccination history, microchip information, collars, leashes, id tags, medication, pet food and a favorite blanket or toy. For cats, put the pet bag into a cat carrier so that the carrier is ready to go when needed. Try to place the pet bag in a safe location, such as with a friend or family member or secure outdoor location.
- Have photos of your pets and any instructions on feeding or caring for your pets.
- To prove ownership of your pet, it is important to have vet records, adoption receipts, etc in your name. If you do not have those records, have your pet examined by a vet before leaving so that any records are in your name. Once you leave the home, consider changing clinics so that you and your pet cannot be tracked.
- If seeking a protective order, be sure to ask that pets are included in the order. Many states have specific laws that allow the inclusion of pets, but a judge can add a pet to the order upon request and showing cause.

On-site housing, Off-site Housing, and Community Programs for people and pets who need a safe escape from domestic violence: https://safeplaceforpets.org/

Pet assistance for low income individuals and/or families, homeless who own pets, victims of domestic violence: http://starelief.org/our-programs/

Shelters equipped to accept families of domestic violence along with their pets: https://alliephillips.com/saf-tprogram/saf-t-shelters/

Pet technology safety and stalking: https://www.techsafety.org/smart-toys?rq=pet

- Food and water dispensers are being combined with cameras and speakers so that owners can check in on their pets when they are away, even playing with them through the device or tossing a treat.
- Some devices track a pet's location or vital signs, relaying the information over the Internet or via an app.
- As with devices for children, location tracking devices for pets were previously based on GPS technology. Newer devices use more energy-efficient, longer-lasting technologies paired with the convenience of a connection to a mobile device or web interface. These devices, like smart toys, often have inadequate security features, or do not encourage owners to change default security settings. The devices could be used to monitor the home through a camera or track the location of the person while walking their pet, for example.

Appendix G

Scripture for Prayer and Meditation

The following are some Scriptures to meditate on and pray over yourself and your children. They are paraphrased and I wrote most of them in the plural for you and your children. Of course modify for whatever your need is!

Thank you, Father, for Your promise that whatever I ask for in prayer, believing, it is granted. I receive as my present possession the things which I am praying for, being assured that as I am praying Your Word, I am praying Your will. (Mark 11:24; I John 5:14-15)

Thank you that as Your Word goes out of my mouth, it is not returning to You void or producing no effect, but it is accomplishing that which You please and purpose, and it is prospering in the thing for which You sent it. (Isaiah 55:11)

As I pray Your Word, You have promised that You will do whatever I ask in Your name, so You will be glorified through Your Son. You also say You have exalted above all else Your name and Your Word, and that You have magnified Your Word above all Your name! So Father, I not only pray in the name of Jesus today, but I pray

Your Word, knowing You will honor Your Word even above all Your name. (John 14:13; Psalm 138:2)

Children

Thank you, Father, that You, the God of peace, are strengthening, completing, perfecting and making my children what they ought to be. You are equipping them with everything good that they may carry out Your will; while You Yourself work in them and accomplish that which pleases You. (Hebrews 13:20-21)

Your Holy Spirit rests upon my children; the spirit of wisdom and understanding, the spirit of counsel and might, the spirit of knowledge and the reverential and obedient fear of the Lord. You are making them of quick understanding, and their delight is in the fear of the Lord. They do not judge by sight, neither do they decide by hearing, but they judge with righteous judgment. (Isaiah 11:2-4)

Father, I declare that my children are being filled with the full knowledge of Your will, in all spiritual wisdom into Your ways and purposes; and in understanding and discernment of spiritual things. They are living and conducting themselves in a manner worthy of You, pleasing to You, and desiring to please You in all things. They are bearing fruit in every good work and growing and increasing in the knowledge of You. They are being invigorated and strengthened with all power according to the might of Your glory and exercising every kind of endurance and patience with joy. (Colossians 1:9-11)

Thank you that You are remembering Your covenant with my children and You are establishing an everlasting covenant with them. As You have thought and planned concerning my children, so shall it happen. As You have purposed for my children, so shall it stand; for what You have purposed, who can annul it? When Your hand is stretched out, who will turn it back? What You speak is done. What You command stands fast. You bring the counsel of corrupt people to nothing; You make the thoughts and plans of wicked people to no effect. Your counsel stands forever; the thoughts of Your heart to all generations. My children have many plans in their minds, and other people may have plans for them, but it is Your purpose for them that will stand. (Ezekiel 16:60; Isaiah 14:24, 27; Proverbs 19:2; Psalm 33:9-11)

Thank you that You are granting out of the rich treasury of Your glory, that my children are strengthened and reinforced with the mighty power of the Holy Spirit indwelling their innermost beings and personalities. Christ, through their faith, is making His permanent home in their hearts. They are rooted and founded on love. Therefore, they have the power to apprehend with all the saints, the experience of that love—the breadth and length and height and depth. They are coming to know through experience for themselves, the love of Christ, which surpasses mere knowledge without experience. As a result, they are being filled through all their being with Your fullness. They have the richest measure of Your Divine Presence and are becoming filled and flooded with Your love. (Ephesians 3:16-19)

You have not given my children a spirit of fear, but of power, authority, love, a calm well-balanced mind, discipline and self-control. They do not shrink back in shame to testify for You and for the truth. (2 Timothy 1:7-8)

Thank you for changing my family's impure language and giving us a clear and pure speech from pure lips. We are calling on Your name, serving You in unity, bearing the yoke of the Lord. As for me and my house, we are serving You Lord. (Zephaniah 3:9; Joshua 24:15)

Protect my children, Father God. Preserve my children from wicked and violent people who plan evil things in their hearts and whose speech is as the venom of vipers. Give us discernment over who these people are who want to hurt my children. Guard my kids from those who would plan to snare them in their nets. (Psalm 140:1-5)

Father, I declare that I am not ashamed, nor is my face pale with fear and disappointment because of my children's degeneracy. For I see my children walking in the ways of virtue, with the work of Your hands in their midst. They revere and love You. Those who erred in spirit are coming to understanding, and those who murmured are accepting instruction. (Jeremiah 29:22-24)

Harmony

Father, fill up our dwelling with Your peace and joy. May we live in harmony with each other, having the same mind and purpose. Help us to not do anything from selfishness, strife or for unworthy ends, but instead with a true spirit of humility regard each other as better than ourselves, showing affection and compassionate sympathy. (Philippians 2:1-3)

Thank you Father, for bringing my family into the same mind, that we sympathize with and love each other, and are compassionate, kind and courteous toward each other. (1 Peter 3:8)

Parenting

I can do all things through Christ Jesus who strengthens me and gives me sufficiency for every task. (Philippians 4:13)

I will not fret or have anxiety about anything, but in every circumstance and in everything by prayer and thanksgiving, will make my requests known to God. Thank you, Father that Your peace that transcends all understanding guards my heart and mind in Christ Jesus. (Philippians 4:6-7)

Father, I declare that the Spirit of Elijah is turning and reconciling the hearts of my children to me, and my heart to them. My children obey me in the Lord. They honor, esteem and value me as precious, and as a result, all is well with them and they shall live long on the earth. I have confidence that my children are doing the things

I wisely suggest and charge them to do. (Malachi 4:5-6; Ephesians 6:1-3; 2 Thessalonians 3:4)

Thank you Father, that the only work which You require of me as a mother is to believe in Your son Jesus. Therefore, I claim Your promise that my work shall be rewarded. By faith, I declare that my children are returning from the enemy's land. There is hope in my future. My children are coming again to their own country. (John 6:28-29; Jeremiah 31:16-17)

Victory

Thank you Father for ransoming my children and myself unharmed from the battle waged against us. We cast all our cares upon You and thank You for sustaining us. (Psalm 55:18,22)

I build up the wall and stand in the gap on behalf of my children. I loose the chains of injustice and untie the cords of the yoke to set the oppressed free and break every yoke. I bind the powers of darkness that come against my children and me and I loose the powers of the kingdom of God in our lives. Thank you, that the angel of the Lord encamps around us and delivers us. (Ezekiel 22:30; Isaiah 58:6; Matthew 18:18; Psalm 34:7)

Thank you, Father that my children and I lack no good thing. You are our confidence and will keep our feet from being snared. We will not fear bad news because our hearts are steadfast, trusting in You. (Psalm 112:7, 34:9-10; Proverbs 3:26)

Father, I declare that my children do not unequally yoke themselves with the ungodly and abusive. They do not come under bondage with those whose lives are inconsistent with their faith. If my children are put under a yoke of bondage, I trust You to protect them and set them free from it. (2 Corinthians 6:14)

Father, I ask You to deliver my children from corrupt and evil companions and influences. Bring them to the knowledge of the truth and help them escape out of the snare of the devil that has held them captive so that they may do Your will. May my children walk as companions of the wise and therefore be wise. (2 Timothy 2:25-26; Proverbs 13:20; 1 Corinthians 15:33-34)

Father, I pray that when my children hear Your voice, and hear truth, they do not harden their hearts. Open their eyes to what is truth and protect them from lies and deception. Lead them into all truth. Cause them to recall and bring to their remembrance everything that is of truth. (Hebrew 4:7; John 14:26)

I declare that my children are disciples, taught of You and obedient to Your will. Great is their peace and undisturbed composure. They are establishing themselves on righteousness. They are far from the thought of oppression or destruction. They do not fear. They are far from terror, for it does not come near them. He who stirs up strife against us is failing away to us. No weapon that is formed against us is prospering. Every tongue that rises against us in judgment we are showing to be in the wrong. (Isaiah 54:13-17)

Father, I declare that every purpose or undertaking that is of human or demonic origin in our lives is failing, being overthrown and coming to nothing. Every purpose or undertaking that is of YOU is not able to be stopped, overthrown or destroyed. (Acts 5:38-39)

Protection

I submit myself under the authority of the Lord Jesus Christ and I bind all demonic forces that are trying to hinder me and my children from being in the will of God. I claim by faith that we are surrounded by a hedge of protection, a wall of fire, and a wall of faith all covered under the blood of Jesus. (James 4:6-7; 1 Peter 5:6-9; Matthew 16:19; Revelation 7:1; Hosea 2:6; Zechariah 2:5)

I bind all demonic forces by the blood of the Lamb and pray

that Jesus would send holy angels to stop any evil assignment against my children and myself. By faith I release the working power of the resurrected Lord and the Holy Spirit in our lives. By faith I claim that every evil assignment has been bound in heaven and thank You that You will guide us into the center of Your will and show us the works You have planned for us. (Hebrew 1:14; Romans 6:4; Ephesians 5:18; Matthew 18:18; John 16:13)

Father, I thank You for causing confusion in the camp of our enemies so that we may have victory over them. Thank you for victory over every trial. Send Your messengers and the provision that we need to accomplish Your will. Give us knowledge and wisdom to know and do Your will. Fill us with the power of the Holy Spirit and give us the fruit of the Spirit to accomplish Your will. (Psalm 35:4, 26; 1 Corinthians 15:57; Luke 6:38; Ephesians 1:17-19; Galatians 5:22-23)

Father, I declare that my children and I shall not die, but live, and declare Your works and illustrious acts. (Psalm 118:17)

I declare that my children and I dwell in a peaceable habitation, in a safe dwelling and in a quiet resting place. (Isaiah 32:18)

Thank you, Father, that You are instructing my children and I and teaching us in the way that we should go. You are counseling us with Your eye upon us. You are delivering and drawing us unto Yourself from every assault of evil. You are preserving and bringing us safe to Your heavenly kingdom. (Psalm 32:8; II Timothy 4:18)

Father, because I have made You my dwelling place and my refuge, I trust that no evil shall befall my children or me, that no plague will come near our dwelling place. Command Your angels to guard us and bear us up. In Your strength, we will tread upon the lion and adder. As a mother of Your children, I rest on Your promise, *"I will rescue those who love me. I will protect those who trust in my name. When they call on me I will answer; I will be with them in trouble. I will rescue and honor them. I will reward them with long life and give them my salvation."* (Psalm 91:9-16)

Provision

We receive from God whatever we ask of Him because we watchfully and habitually practice what is pleasing to Him. My children and I live in Him and His words are in our heart, therefore we ask whatever we will and it will be done for us. (1 John 3:22; John 15:7)

The Lord is our sun and shield and He bestows grace, favor and honor on us. No good thing does He withhold from us because we walk uprightly. He liberally supplies all our needs according to His riches in glory in Christ Jesus. We bring everything to Him in prayer with thanksgiving, and the peace of God, which passes all understanding, keeps our heart and mind through Christ Jesus. (Psalm 84:11; Philippians 4:6-7,19)

Healing

Thank you, Jesus for bearing my grief and carrying my sorrow. You were stricken, smitten of God and afflicted that I and my children may have life. You were wounded for our transgressions and bruised for our iniquities. The chastisement of our peace was upon You, and by Your stripes we are healed. I receive Jesus as my Healer just as I have received Him as my Savior. The power to resist sickness resides in me. (Isaiah 53:4-5)

My children and I walk in divine health and life, for Jesus has conquered sickness in our life. Thank you Jesus for taking our sickness on Your body, and that by Your suffering we are healed. Divine health pulsates through every cell of our body, overcoming sickness and disease. (2 Peter 1:4; Matthew 8:17)

Heal us Lord, and we shall be healed; save us and we shall be saved, for You are our praise. I thank You that it is Your will that in our lives every unclean spirit is cast out, and every disease and affliction is healed. You deliver us in the day of trouble; You protect us and keep us alive. You do not give us up to the will of our enemies. You sustain us through sickness and restore us to full health. (Jeremiah 17:14; Matthew 10:1; Psalm 41:1-3)

Thank you, Father for healing our broken hearts and binding up our wounds. You bring us health and healing and reveal to us abundance of prosperity and security. We will not forget You and all Your benefits. You forgive us all our iniquity, heal all our diseases, redeem our lives from destruction, and crown us with Your steadfast love and mercy. (Jeremiah 33:6; Psalm 103:2-4)

Courage

Thank you, Father for giving my children and I strength and boldness. We will not live in fear or dread, because You go with us everywhere we go and we have confidence that You will never fail us nor forsake us. We will be strong and courageous. We will not come under the dominion of fear and dismay, for You did not give us a spirit of fear and timidity, but a spirit of power, love and a strong mind. (Deuteronomy 31:6-8; 2 Timothy 1:7)

Because we love and worship You alone God, we can be strong and courageous to face every battle in front of us. We will not be terrified or discouraged, for You are with us wherever we go. We are on our guard, standing firm in our faith in You, full of great courage and strength and wisdom. (Joshua 1:9-10; 1 Corinthians 16:13)

We trust in the Lord with all our heart and do not rely on our own understanding. In all our ways we acknowledge Him and He makes our paths straight. We have no fear of bad news. Our hearts are steadfast, trusting in the Lord. (Proverbs 3:5; Psalm 112:7)

Peace

We will lie down and sleep in peace; for You alone Lord make my children and me lie down in safety. You speak peace to us because we are faithful to You and turn to You with all our hearts. Your steadfast love, faithfulness, righteousness and peace fill us and surround us. Because we love you, we abide in great peace and nothing can make us stumble. (Psalm 4:8, 85:8,10, 119:165)

Thank you, Father, for causing us to please You and that You cause our enemies to be at peace with us. You ordain peace for us, keeping our minds in perfect peace because we trust in You. (Proverbs 16:7; Isaiah 26:3)

You lead us in paths of righteousness and cause us to dwell in a peaceful habitation, in secure dwellings and in quiet resting places. We enjoy the result of righteousness which is quietness and trust forever. (Isaiah 32:17-18)

Thank you, Father, that though the mountains may depart and the hills be removed, Your steadfast love and covenant of peace shall not be removed from my children or I. You have compassion on us and lead us forth in joy and back in peace. (Isaiah 54:10-12)

Exercise A

What Are Your Values?

Your values are what is important to you in life. By building a life and lifestyle around your values you create a life that is more satisfying and meaningful. Values change over time and deepen as you understand yourself better.

INSTRUCTIONS

1. What are your top 5 values? Circle them or write them down.

2. On a scale of 1 - 10, with 10 representing its highest value to you, how important is each one? Write that number beside each value.

3. Now, on a scale of 1 - 10, how would you score yourself LIVING this value? If your number for this one is lower than the previous number you wrote down, why do you think that is? What can you do to bring this number up so that you can live true to yourself?

Column 1	Column 2	Column 3
Accomplishment	Enthusiasm	Loyalty
Accuracy	Excellence	Optimism
Acknowledgment	Fairness	Orderliness
Adventure	Flexibility	Participation
Authenticity	Focus	Partnership
Balance	Forgiveness	Passion
Beauty	Friendship	Patience
Boldness	Fun	Peace
Calm	Generosity	Presence
Challenge	Gentleness	Productivity
Collaboration	Growth	Respect
Community	Happiness	Resourcefulness
Compassion	Harmony	Romance
Comradeship	Health	Safety
Confidence	Helpfulness	Service
Connectedness	Honesty	Simplicity
Contentment	Honor	Spirituality
Contribution	Humor	Spontaneity
Cooperation	Idealism	Strength
Courage	Independence	Tact
Creativity	Innovation	Thankfulness
Curiosity	Integrity	Tolerance
Determination	Intuition	Tradition
Directness	Joy	Trust
Discovery	Kindness	Understanding
Ease	Learning	Unity
Effortlessness	Listening	Vitality
Empowerment	Love	Wisdom

Exercise B

Draw Out Your Gremlin

A "gremlin" stops you from achieving your goals in life. It is an *internal habit or feeling* that seems to run on its own accord. It rises up and stops you from taking action. Awareness of your gremlin gives you the opportunity to make changes and do things differently. By acknowledging your gremlin and questioning its validity, you gain wisdom and learn the lessons needed to bypass it. For example, common gremlins are self-sabotage, fear of conflict, fear of failure, and fear of dreaming.

INSTRUCTIONS

1. Draw a picture of what your gremlin looks like. No need to be fancy and don't judge yourself - just draw! Your gremlin might have characteristics of a parent or authority figure from your past. If you feel stuck, start drawing without thinking about it, or use your non-dominant hand. Feel free to add phrases your gremlin uses such as, "You should have known better," or "You're not good enough."

2. Review your gremlin. What do you notice about your drawing? Is there a critical frown or piercing eyes looking for

mistakes, etc. Write down key gremlin features and what they represent.

a. When is your gremlin most active? Where and when does it tend to pop up? What's happening at the time?

b. What is your gremlin's purpose? What is it trying to achieve?

c. What is your gremlin MOST afraid of?

d. Where does your gremlin come from? What specific people or experiences?

e. If your gremlin had a name, what would it be?

f. Who would you be without this gremlin?

g. How could your life change and improve if you were to let go of this gremlin?

h. Finally, what will you do with this information? What ONE action will you take?

"If you hear a voice within you say 'you cannot paint,' then by all means paint, and that voice will be silenced."

~Vincent Van Gogh

Exercise C

Calm the "Monkey Mind"

We all get "Monkey Mind" from time to time. Our minds roam out of control, swinging from one thing to the next. Sometimes it's exciting: plans we are making, ideas we have. Other times it can be a long catalog of things to remember, worries and "shoulds." Often it's a mix of both. Of course the worst time to have "Monkey Mind" is when you are trying to get to sleep. This exercise calms down the mind so you can get the rest you deserve!

INSTRUCTIONS

1. Simply write down ANY and EVERY thing that's on your mind. Literally. Just put pen to paper and write. And no judgment! The only rule is that there are no rules. Whatever pops up, write it down. *E.g. Great ideas; what to have for breakfast; a feeling, memory, grievance; worry that you need a haircut; to see the dentist or something else.*

2. Keep writing until your brain is exhausted of things to tell you about.

3. Then ask, "If there was something/s I missed, what would it be?" Write these down.

4. Pause and take a look at the things on your 'Monkey Mind' list.

5. Let go of your 'Cheeky Monkeys': These are items you have no control over, there is nothing you can do. Cross these items out. Take a deep breath and let go of each for now.

6. Identify your 'Gorillas': Circle the items that are really bothering you or that your mind keeps going back to - whatever it is - however big, small, silly, boring or illogical it may or may not be!

7. Look at the 'Gorilla' items you've circled and pick an action for each that you will (ideally) take tomorrow. *E.g. Phone dentist/hair salon, buy milk, brainstorm business/holiday ideas over lunch, research personal trainers, call mom, set up meeting with school, etc.*

8. Now check in with yourself. How busy is your mind now? _____ / 10.

Once your mind busy-ness score is 2 (or less) out of 10, wonderful! Take a deep breath. Acknowledge and thank your brain for all these great thoughts and review your action plan one final time.

If your mind busy-ness score is 3 or above, ask yourself: "What haven't I mentioned yet that needs to be seen, felt or heard?"

Then just keep writing until you're done. Look at your new item/s. What can you do about it, however small? If there is something, add it to your action list, otherwise cross out your 'Cheeky Monkeys' as before.

Keep going until your score is 2 or less, out of 10.

TIP: If you want your brain to calm, it needs to know you are listening. Your action doesn't have to be big. It can be the smallest step you could take. But commit to yourself and do it as soon as you can. And remember your action could also be to let it go.

Exercise D

Detox Your Toxic Relationships

Over the course of our lives we spend most of our time with just 5 people!

Success experts say that WHO we spend our time with is a key influence on our happiness and whether we succeed or fail. Experience shows that happy, successful people spend most of their time with other people who are happy and successful.

What better time than now to identify those people who inspire and lead you into better things, and to notice those people who pull you down? This exercise will bring this information to the forefront where you'll naturally start making different choices about who you spend your time with.

INSTRUCTIONS

1. Make a list of the 20 people you spend most of your time with. Against each one put a:

    + if you feel good about yourself after spending time with them. You enjoy your time with them, and they are happy and successful in their own way. These are often people you *look forward* to spending time with.

- if you find after spending time with them you *somehow* feel 'less.' Perhaps you feel smaller, less happy or have less energy. These may be people where you may worry or stress unnecessarily before or after seeing them. You probably already have a gut feeling who these people are.

2. Add a gut-feeling score from -5 to +5 against each person to identify HOW much of an effect they have on you.
3. Finally, for the people who have the highest and lowest scores, write an action for what you can do to increase or decrease their involvement in your life.

COMMON FIRST SIGNS OF A TOXIC PERSON (YELLOW FLAG)

- Bad-mouths others
- Complains
- Expects special treatment
- Boasts
- Puts you on the defensive
- Makes you work to please them
- Uninterested in your concerns
- Inconsistent
- Manipulative

COMMON SIGNS OF DANGEROUS PERSONALITIES (RED FLAG)

- Charming
- Habit of lying

- Unsympathetic
- Deliberately provoking and misleading people
- Manipulative
- Does what is personally convenient or rewarding
- Massive ego
- Does not respect other people's time
- Secretive about themselves
- Controlling
- Denies the facts
- Plays victim card to avoid blame
- Volatile temper
- Belittles others, does not respect others
- Risk taking
- Gives misleading information
- Takes pleasure in pitting people against each other, causing discomfort

SOME DIFFERENCES BETWEEN NICE AND GOOD (nice does not equal good!)

Nice

- A person is worthwhile as long as beneficial
- Says what you want to hear/flatters
- Lacks genuine apologies and forgiveness
- Flamboyant
- Prince Charming and makes careless promises
- When needed isn't available
- Rushes things

Good

- Cautious/thoughtful to avoid causing unnecessary hardship
- Treats everyone with respect regardless
- Says (with kindness) what you need to hear
- Apologizes and forgives
- Concerned more with inner character
- Knows limitations and doesn't make empty promises
- Is there for you even when it's inconvenient

GASLIGHTING is psychological manipulation that seeks to cause you to question your own memory, perception and sanity. A form of mental and emotional abuse that makes you unsure of yourself and more dependent on them.

- I was just joking
- I didn't do that
- You're imagining things
- You make stuff up in your head
- Don't be so sensitive
- You have issues
- You're upset over nothing
- Stop imagining things
- You need help
- I never said that
- No one likes you
- They're lying
- Here we go again
- I don't have time for this

- You have selective memory
- There's always drama with you
- It's always something with you
- You're reading too much into it
- OTHER people like me, it's JUST YOU that has a negative view/opinion of me

BLAME-SHIFTING is when a person does something wrong or inappropriate, and then dumps the blame on you to avoid taking responsibility for their own behavior.

- Plays the victim. You ask him to stop ridiculing you, so he accuses you of something hurtful so you end up the one doing the apologizing. He may also use the pity-party tactic by bringing up his traumatic childhood or evil ex so that you end up comforting him and understanding why he is that way. No more responsibility!

- Minimizes your feelings. You express how hurt you were over his comment. He minimizes your feelings (see gas-lighting section) so that your response to his original comment is now the misbehavior.

- Argues the argument. He attacks your words, tone, semantics to shift the blame onto you for the way you approached the argument. (See victim playing, gas-lighting, projection)

- Accusation. Maybe you have gathered the evidence and there is no way he's getting out of it. So he accuses you of abuse, cheating, mental illness, stalking…

WHAT MAKES YOU A GOOD TARGET

- You give trust without the other person earning it
- You are empathetic and tend to see the good in everyone

- You rationalize or ignore red flags and your own instincts

What to do instead:
- Accept that there are people who have no conscience or compulsion to care for others and they seem like nice people who are often accomplished.
- Acknowledge the signs that are there and be honest with yourself about it. You are not to blame and you can't fix it.
- Fight toxicity with positivity.
- Balance out their presence (if you can't get away) with other more positive people or solitary relaxation time.
- Don't engage if possible. Keep quiet and walk away.
- Limit the information you share.
- Know your limits and set boundaries with consequences. Follow through when they are tested.
- Don't take it personally - their behavior is a reflection of them, not you.
- If it becomes physical (married or otherwise) it's a legal matter that needs dealt with.
- Practice self-care daily. Put your needs first. (See Exercise F & G)
- Educate yourself on passive-aggression, gas-lighting, emotional abuse, etc so you recognize the tactics.
- Recognize your desire to "rescue" and stop taking the bait. You don't have to rescue them or fix their drama.
- You don't have to justify, argue, explain or defend yourself - it just sets you up for a fall because he wants you to react so he can use your reaction to prove his point.

- DO NOT isolate yourself from people who care and can support you through this. A support system is vital.
- Create an exit plan. (See Appendix D)
- Severely abusive relationships need to be handled differently to ensure your safety. If you are in immediate danger, call 9-1-1. For anonymous, confidential help, 24/7, please call the National Domestic Violence Hotline at 1-800-799-7233 (SAFE) or 1-800-787-3224 (TTY).

You deserve to be happy. You deserve to live a life you are excited about. Don't let others make you forget that. If someone doesn't respect, value and appreciate you, then she/he doesn't deserve to be a part of your life!

Exercise E

No More Excuses

INSTRUCTIONS

Are you getting in your own way? Are you making excuses for not taking action? It takes courage and honesty to admit we make excuses, even though we ALL do it… While making excuses can be a good thing, it also undermines our confidence in ourselves and life itself. Awareness is power! Simply use the exercise below to identify your excuses, understand the underlying fear/consequences, and commit to do things differently.

1. Start by writing out the goal or outcome you are looking for.
2. Next pick 3-5 excuses you make on a regular basis. (Examples might be, I'm too busy… I don't have… I'm too tired. Look for words like "can't," "don't have," "didn't," "sorry but," or "because.")
3. For each excuse, answer the following questions:
    a. What's the underlying thought or fear? (What's really going on? Write whatever thought or feeling comes to mind no matter how silly it seems.)

b. What's the cost/impact of this excuse? (How specifically does this excuse affect you, your life, relationships?)

c. What could I say instead? (What would you like to hear yourself say instead? How could you be kind to yourself and still move toward your goal?)

d. What will I do with this information? (What will you do to address your excuse making?)

Why We Make Excuses:

- We make excuses when we're simply not motivated enough. We tend to be more motivated to avoid or move away from pain and discomfort than towards goals and pleasure.

- Making excuses is a self-protection mechanism. By making an excuse we protect ourselves from feelings of shame, guilt, anxiety, embarrassment, fear and discomfort.

- Excuses help us shift the focus from something deeply personal to something more general e.g. It's easier to say, "I was too tired" or "I changed my mind" than acknowledge our deep fear of failure.

Some Common Reasons We Make Excuses:

- Fear; of failure, success, embarrassment or ridicule, uncertainty or change, making a mistake, responsibility, upsetting others or a general fear of the feelings evoked when we think about our goal!

- Limiting beliefs; a lack of belief in our ability to follow through or complete, and that things will not work out.

- Uncertainty; a lack of clarity about the outcomes or what might be involved in making the change.

- Lack of readiness; we may lack information, time, energy or some other resource to make the change.

- It's not really our goal; the goal may be a "should" or we're doing it to please someone else.
- Avoiding discomfort; of making change or how others will react to what we want to do.
- Complications; we start the process and find it's harder or more involved than we first thought, and are now uncertain if we want to proceed.
- Inertia; it's much easier to stay where we are and not do something than take a risk and make the effort to change.

When Making Excuses Is Helpful:

- Excuses can be helpful when they: 1) Preserve the original goal and 2) are made with compassion and understanding. This kind of excuse making preserves our self-esteem and helps us feel good about giving it another go.

The Impact of Excuse-Making:

- When we regularly make excuses rather than take action towards our goals damages our self-esteem. We reinforce unchallenged fears and limiting beliefs, block our creativity and disappoint others and ourselves.
- In addition, when we make excuses to others we can damage how others perceive us.
- Ultimately, making habitual excuses can lead to a more negative view of life, carrying around regrets and generally leading a less satisfying life.

The Answer to Excuse Making:

- The answer is not to stop making excuses but to raise our awareness and be honest with ourselves. It's essential to be kind. If we're harsh with ourselves, it's not going to inspire us to make change and step outside our comfort zones. Instead we need to change what we say and what we do when we feel the familiar excuse coming on.

Making Change:

- Research shows that while it can become a habit to make excuses, even a short pause can be enough to catch ourselves and focus on the outcomes we want instead of avoiding our fears and discomfort.
- Changing our excuses can be challenging, as it involves facing our deepest selves. Often when we look at the underlying reasons for our excuses we judge ourselves. We know we could do something, we're "just" afraid or are "lazy" and don't want to face the discomfort.
- No-one performs better when feeling judged and under scrutiny and this is why kindness is key.

The purpose of this exercise is to raise your awareness around the excuses you commonly make, so that you can be kinder to yourself and make more conscious choices.

Exercise F

How Is Your Self-Care?

INSTRUCTIONS

How good are you to yourself? Let's find out! There are no right or wrong answers, just answer however seems appropriate for you right now and see what you learn about yourself.

Scoring: Score 2 points for each Yes, 1 point for each Sometimes, and 0 points for No's.

1. I am up-to-date with my optician, dentist and other health check-ups.

Y S N

2. I am happy with my physical fitness and energy levels.

Y S N

3. I eat nutritionally most of the time and do not abuse my body with caffeine, alcohol or similar.

Y S N

4. I get plenty of sleep most of the time.

Y S N

5. I take regular breaks from my work during the day, at weekends and use holidays for enjoyment & relaxation.

Y S N

6. I like how my hair is and am happy with my wardrobe and 'style.'

Y S N

7. I meditate, journal, relax or have me-time regularly (where I am not doing chores or things for others.)

Y S N

8. I prioritize how I spend my time and important things get done in time.

Y S N

9. I say "no" when I need or want to.

Y S N

10. My home is cleaned regularly to a standard I am happy with.

Y S N

11. My home is organized and tidy and somewhere I love to be.

Y S N

12. My home is a calm haven (or has a place within it) that takes me away from the stresses of the world.

Y S N

13. I recognize my stress signals and know when to take a break.

Y S N

14. I have people in my life who love and support me.

Y S N

15. Apart from my job or exceptional situations, I only spend time with people who support, energize and inspire me.

Y S N

16. I listen to and trust my intuition when it comes to taking care of myself.

Y S N

17. I have a mentor/s that support and encourage me in life.

Y S N

18. I have forgiven myself my past mistakes.

Y S N

19. I have let go of resentments towards others.

Y S N

20. I have things that help my life run smoothly (anything from contact lens solution to pens, paper, vitamins or bathroom tissue!)

Y S N

21. I have things to look forward to in my life.

Y S N

The maximum possible total is 42. Write your total score here: ___

What did you learn about yourself?

Go to Exercise G for ideas to take better care of yourself.

Exercise G

Daily Self-Care Guide

To sustain yourself through difficult changes, you need to practice good self-care. Sleep deprivation, poor nutrition, personal conflicts, financial concerns, and no private time decreases your ability to manage your life in a satisfying way. Complete the following exercise to set your day up for success and create desired long-term change by making small daily changes. Take a few minutes either in the morning or before bed to write your answers and then review them at the end of the day and celebrate your successes! Even if you only accomplish one, it counts as cause to celebrate!

- 5 things I am grateful for:
- A compliment to myself today:
- 2 favors to do for myself today:
- One new thing I would like to try: How? When?
- Something I learned recently:
- One mind-set shift I want to work on today: (Example: I want to change my thought of "I can't meet new people" to "I can smile and say something to a stranger at the grocery store today.")

- A boundary I need to set today:
- What is urgent to do today:
- What is an "I ideally would like to do today":
- One change to improve my environment today: (Example: pick up the magazines cluttering the table)
- One change to improve my physical health today: (Example: eat a salad)
- One change to improve my mental/emotional health today: (Example: turn off the news and instead listen to uplifting music)
- One change to improve my finances today: (Example: put $10 in a secret savings account)
- One change to improve my relationships: (Example: go through Exercise D to detox my relationships)
- What I really want: (Are you moving toward or away from what you really want?)

Resources

HELPLINES (Accessed February 2019)

It can be dangerous to try to teach an abuser about DV by sharing books & information. Instead, please read the resources listed and find a support group. Call 1-800-799-SAFE (U.S.) 24/7 for support, safe shelter & referrals to free support groups, counseling, legal help and children's services.

Pathways to Safety International 1-833-SAFE-833 https://pathwaystosafety.org/

Love is Respect 1-866-331-9474 http://www.loveisrespect.org/

National Center on Elder Abuse 1-855-500-3537 https://ncea.acl.gov/

National Center for Victims of Crime 1-855-4-VICTIM http://www.victimsofcrime.org/

National Child Abuse Hotline 1-800-4-A-CHILD https://www.childhelp.org/hotline/

National Clearinghouse for the Defense of Battered Women 1-800-903-0111 x3 (Accepts collect calls from incarcerated victims of battering.) http://www.ncdbw.org/

National Coalition against Domestic Violence 1-800-799-SAFE or 1-800-787-3224 (TTY) http://www.ncadv.org/

National Coalition for the Homeless 1-202-462-4822 http://www.nationalhomeless.org/

National Domestic Violence Hotline 1-800-799-7233 or 1-800-787-3224 (TTY) http://www.thehotline.org/

National Suicide Prevention Lifeline 1-800-273-8255 http://www.suicidepreventionlifeline.org/

RAINN (Rape, Abuse and Incest National Network) 1-800-656-HOPE https://rainn.org/index.php

WEBSITES (accessed February 2019)

God Hates Abuse Project https://www.godhatesabuse.org/

Julie Owens https://www.domesticviolenceexpert.org/

Womens Law http://www.womenslaw.org/

Mosaic Threat Assessment https://www.mosaicmethod.com/

Pandora's Project http://www.pandys.org/index.html

Bursting the Bubble (teens and young adults) http://www.burstingthebubble.com/

Domestic Shelters https://www.domesticshelters.org/

RAVE http://www.theraveproject.com/index.php

GRACE Godly Response to Abuse in the Christian Environment http://www.netgrace.org/

Courageous Kids Network http://www.courageouskids.net/

PJ Lambert https://pjlambert.com/

Taffy Hunter Mathison https://littlebirdflies.wordpress.com/

Shine a Light on Domestic Violence Ministry https://www.shinealightondv.org/

Changing Men Changing Lives http://www.changingmenchanginglives.org/

Divorce Care https://www.divorcecare.org/

Protective Mothers' Alliance International http://protectivemothersallianceinternational.org/

Children Against Court Appointed Child Abuse http://ca3cacaca.blogspot.com/

Manipulative People http://www.manipulative-people.com/

Safe Relationships Magazine https://saferelationshipsmagazine.com/

Navigating Uncharted Waters https://annecarolinedrake.com/

Safe-at-last's Survival Guide For Victims Of Family Violence & Domestic Abuse http://hubpages.com/relationships/Domestic-Violence-OK-So-its-Abuse-What-Now

BIFF Response (respond to hostile emails, texts and other communications) https://www.highconflictinstitute.com/biff-responses/

The Cycle of Abuse Wheel http://storage.cloversites.com/abuserecoveryministryservices/documents/abuse%20cycle_2.pdf

Lundy Bancroft http://www.lundybancroft.com/ http://lundybancroft.blogspot.com/

Prevent Abusive Relationships http://www.preventabusiverelationships.com/index.php

Focus Ministries http://www.focusministries1.org/

The Mordecai Project https://themordecaiproject.org/

Girls Gone Wise http://www.girlsgonewise.com/

Faith Trust Institute http://www.faithtrustinstitute.org/

A Cry for Justice http://cryingoutforjustice.com/

Sanctuary for the Abused http://abusesanctuary.blogspot.com/

The Mama Bear Effect http://themamabeareffect.org/

Blues Behind Bars https://www.livingfirearts.org/page4 (Ministry by David and Lisa Boyd to inmates. Their song-writing workshop produces inspirational songs written by inmates about their personal experience with domestic violence. You can also listen to the songs on SoundCloud.)

ARTICLES (accessed February 2019)

Assessing Risk to Children from Batterers by Lundy Bancroft http://www.lundybancroft.com/

The Batterer as Parent by Lundy Bancroft http://www.lundybancroft.com/

Understanding the Batterer in Custody and Visitation Disputes by Lundy Bancroft http://www.lundybancroft.com/

Safety Planning with Children of Battered Women by Lundy Bancroft http://www.lundybancroft.com/

The Connection between Batterers and Child Sexual Abuse Perpetrators by Lundy Bancroft http://www.lundybancroft.com/

Honouring Resistance: How Women Resist Abuse in Intimate Relationships by Calgary Women's Shelter https://www.calgarywomensshelter.com/images/pdf/cwesResistancebookletfinalweb.pdf

Contrition, Behavior and Therapy by Dr. Simon http://www.manipulative-people.com/

Assessing Dangerousness in Men Who Abuse Women by Lundy Bancroft http://www.lundybancroft.com/

Toxic Relationship Aftermath: Doubt, Mistrust and Paranoia by Dr. Simon http://www.manipulative-people.com/

What's the Difference Between Normal Marital Conflict and Abuse? by Jeff Olson http://questions.org/

Divorced is NOT a Status by Joseph Pote http://josephjpote.com/

BOOKS (in no particular order)

A Cry for Justice: How the Evil of Domestic Abuse Hides in Your Church by Jeff Crippen

Knight in Tarnished Armor by PJ Lambert

A Path to Hope: Restoring the Spirit of the Abused Christian Woman by Rose Saad

Refuge From Abuse by Dr Catherine Clark Kroeger

Not Under Bondage: Biblical Divorce for Abuse, Adultery and Desertion by Barbara Roberts

Why Does He Do That? Inside the Minds of Angry and Controlling Men by Lundy Bancroft

Should I Stay or Should I Go? A Guide to Knowing if your Relationship Can – and Should – be Saved by Lundy Bancroft

Day by Day: Thriving After Sexual Abuse and Trauma by Jan Feil

When Love Hurts by Karen McCandless Davis

Coercive Control by Evan Stark

Unholy Charade: Unmasking the Domestic Abuser in the Church by Jeff Crippen with Rebecca Davis

In Sheep's Clothing: Understanding and Dealing with Manipulative People by George Simon, Jr

The Sociopath Next Door by Martha Stout

Keeping the Faith: Questions and Answers for the Abused Woman by Marie Fortune

The Emotionally Destructive Relationship: Seeing It, Stopping It, Surviving It by Leslie Vernick

Violence Among Us: Ministry to Families in Crisis by Brenda Branson and Paula Silva

A Biblical Perspective of What to Do when You Are Abused by Your Husband by Debi Pryde and Robert Needham

Divorce: God's Will? The Truth of Divorce and Remarriage in the Bible for Christians by Stephen Gola

'Till Death Do Us Part: Love, Marriage, and the Mind of the Killer Spouse by Robi Ludwig and Matt Birbeck

Is It My Fault: Hope and Healing for Those Suffering Domestic Violence by Lindsey Holcomb and Justin Holcomb

Keeping the Faith: Guidance for Christian Women Facing Abuse by Marie Fortune

Sexual Abuse in Christian Homes and Churches by Carolyn Heggen

Addressing Domestic Violence in the Church by Bob Edwards

When Love Goes Wrong by Ann Jones

FACEBOOK (Accessed February 2019)

God Hates Abuse https://www.facebook.com/godhatesabuse/

Julie Owens https://www.facebook.com/groups/AddressingDVinChristianHomes/

Bob Edwards https://www.facebook.com/bob.edwards.letmypeoplego

Biblical Christian Egalitarians https://www.facebook.com/groups/BiblicalChristianEgalitarians/

Give Her Wings to Fly https://www.facebook.com/giveherwingstofly/

Institute for Relational Harm Reduction https://www.facebook.com/InstituteForRelationalHarmReduction/

Southlake Christian Counseling https://www.facebook.com/SouthlakeChristianCounseling/

Freedom from Narcissistic and Emotional Abuse https://www.facebook.com/freedomfromnarcissisticandemotionalabuse/

Keep Kids Free From Abuse https://www.facebook.com/KeepKidsFreefromAbuse/

Pam Lambert https://www.facebook.com/PamelaJeanLambert/

Ezer Rising https://www.facebook.com/EzerRising/

Love is Patient https://www.facebook.com/loveispatientitisnoteasilyangered/

Church Abuse Survivor https://www.facebook.com/churchabusesurvivor/

Childhood Domestic Violence Association https://www.facebook.com/cdv/

Christian Biblical Egalitarians https://www.facebook.com/CBEInt/

Called to Peace https://www.facebook.com/calledtopeace/

Positive Parenting Solutions https://www.facebook.com/PositiveParentingSolutions/

Women With Wings https://www.facebook.com/WomenWithWings2/

SAFETY APPS

Rethink downloading these apps if you feel unsafe, if your (ex) partner monitors you, or makes you feel scared, intimidated or controlled, or helped to set up your phone, had access to your phone, or has linked email or app store accounts with you. *Tech Safety* has in depth information and reviews on safety apps: https://www.techsafety.org/appsafetycenter

SUNNY helps women to recognize, respond and get help if they are experiencing violence and abuse.

ASPIRE NEWS helps hide important information. Hidden in the 'help' section is a list of resources for domestic violence victims. The resources can be notified via a simple click of a button, making it easier than ever to get help in an emergency situation.

BSAFE allows the creation of a social safety network who will be notified if the user feels unsafe.

CIRCLE OF 6 makes it quick and easy to reach the 6 people you choose.

DAISY can link to service phone numbers and websites, which you can access from within the app so they don't show in browser history.

HELP ME has a warning alarm that can be sounded when a person is in danger and send a message to contacts in their safety network.

POSITIVE PATHWAYS is a safety and well-being app for women experiencing domestic and family violence.

PENDA is for women who have experienced domestic and family violence and are thinking about separation and divorce. It contains financial tips, safety and legal information and referrals.

ASK stands for 'Assault, Services, Knowledge' and is a series of apps and websites designed to provide locally specific information to those who have been victims of sexual assault.

TD411 is specifically for teens, providing information on teen dating abuse and healthy relationships.

RUSAFE is a danger assessment app to help users identify if they're in a "dangerous situation," and connect users with local resources.

Works Cited

1. United Nations Office on Drugs and Crime. Global Study on Homicide 2018. http://www.unodc.org/documents/data-and-analysis/GSH2018/GSH18_Gender-related_killing_of_women_and_girls.pdf (accessed February 2019)

2. King, Jeanne. "Abusive Relationships - What Is the Difference between Being Abusive and Being an Abuser?" Prevent Abusive Relationships. http://www.preventabusiverelationships.com/dv_abusive_vs_abuser.html (accessed February 2019).

3. Bancroft, Lundy. *Why Does He Do That? Inside the Minds of Angry and Controlling Men.* New York: Berkley Books, 2003.

4. Bancroft, Lundy. "Understanding & Breaking Free From Relationship Violence - Chat Transcript" Pandora's Project. http://www.pandys.org/lundybancroft-transcript.html (accessed February 2019)

5. Barnes, Albert. "Commentary on Matthew 7" Study Light.

6. Barnes, Albert. "Commentary on Galatians 5" Study Light.

7. Curtis, David. "Judge Not!" Berean Bible Church. http://www.bereanbiblechurch.org/transcripts/matthew/som/7_1-6.htm (accessed February 2019)

8. Curtis, David. "Judge Not!" Berean Bible Church. http://www.

bereanbiblechurch.org/transcripts/matthew/som/7_1-6.htm (accessed February 2019)

9. Crippen, Jeff. "You Cannot Drive Abuse Out of the Abuser" A Cry for Justice. http://cryingoutforjustice.com/2015/11/11/you-cannot-drive-abuse-out-of-the-abuser/ (accessed February 2019)

10. University of St. Thomas. "Biblical Exegesis: 2. Examine the Historical, Cultural, and Literary Background" http://libguides.stthomas.edu/c.php?g=88712&p=573352 (accessed February 2019)

11. Butt, Kyle. "The Biblical View of Women" Apologetics Press. http://www.apologeticspress.org/APContent.aspx?category=13&article=3654 (accessed February 2019)

12. Fortune, Marie. *Keeping the Faith: Questions and Answers for the Abused Woman.* New York: Harper Collins Publishers, 1987.

13. Tracy, Steven. "What Does 'Submit in Everything' Really Mean? The Nature and Scope of Marital Submission" Christians for Biblical Equality. http://www.cbe.org.au/media/docs/SubmitinEverythingTJ.pdf (accessed February 2019)

14. Vernick, Leslie. *The Emotionally Destructive Relationship: Seeing It, Stopping It, Surviving It.* Eugene: Harvest House Publishers, 2007.

15. Grady, J. Lee. "The Dark Side of Wives Submitting to Husbands" Charisma Magazine. http://www.charismamag.com/blogs/fire-in-my-bones/7229-the-dark-side-of-submission (accessed February 2019)

16. Kassian, Mary. "7 Misconceptions about Submission" Girls Gone Wise. http://www.girlsgonewise.com/7-misconceptions-about-submission/ (accessed February 2019)

17. Branson, Brenda, Paula Silva. *Violence Among Us: Ministry to Families in Crisis.* King of Prussia: Judson Press, 2007.

18. Pryde, Debi, Robert Needham. *A Biblical Perspective of What to*

Do when You Are Abused by Your Husband. Newberry Springs: Iron Sharpeneth Iron Publications, 2003.

19. Crippen, Jeff. "Bow Down, Tremble, and Pay Homage!" Sermon Audio.

20. Hallock, Mark. "Part 1: God's Design for Wives" Calvary Church podcast. http://englewood.thecalvary.org/media/sermon-archive/gospel-shaped-family/?sermon_id=148 (accessed February 2019)

21. Tracy, Steven. "What does 'Submit in Everything' Really Mean? The Nature and Scope of Marital Submission" Christians for Biblical Equality. http://www.cbe.org.au/media/docs/SubmitinEverythingTJ.pdf (accessed February 2019)

22. Francisco, Don. "Marriage and Divorce Myth 1 - Does God Hate Divorce?" Rocky Mountain Ministries.

23. Gola, Stephen. *Divorce: God's Will? The Truth of Divorce and Remarriage in the Bible for Christians.* Summerville: Holy Fire Publishing, 2005.

24. Crippen, Jeff. "Marriage, Divorce, and an Ox in a Well" A Cry for Justice. http://cryingoutforjustice.com/2014/06/15/marriage-divorce-and-an-ox-in-a-well/ (accessed February 2019)

25. Fortune, Marie. *Keeping the Faith: Questions and Answers for the Abused Woman.* New York: HarperCollins, 1987.

26. Gola, Stephen. *Divorce: God's Will? The Truth of Divorce and Remarriage in the Bible for Christians.* Summerville: Holy Fire Publishing, 2005.

27. Crippen, Jeff. "How to Deal Properly With Abusers Posing as Christians" A Cry for Justice. http://cryingoutforjustice.com/2015/09/04/how-to-deal-properly-with-abusers-posing-as-christians/ (accessed February 2019)

28. Clanchy, Michael, Chris Trotter. "Infidelity - A Form of Abuse" Sanctuary for the Abused. http://abusesanctuary.blogspot.

com/2006/08/infidelity-form-of-abuse-infidelity.html (accessed February 2019)

29. Crippen, Jeff. "Dealing With the Abuser Part 2" Sermon Audio.

30. Vine, W.E. "Vine's Expository of Dictionary of NT Words" Study Light. http://www.studylight.org/dictionaries/ved/view.cgi?n=45 (accessed February 2019)

31. Ludwig, Robi, Matt Birkbeck. *'Till Death Do Us Part: Love, Marriage, and the Mind of the Killer Spouse.* Atria Books, 2006.

32. Family Violence Prevention Fund. "Predictors of Domestic Violence Homicide" National Center on Domestic and Sexual Violence. http://www.ncdsv.org/images/FWV_PredictorsDVHomicide_2004.pdf (accessed February 2019)

33. Crippen, Jeff. "What About Passive Abuse?" A Cry for Justice. http://cryingoutforjustice.com/2012/04/05/what-about-passive-abuse-by-jeff-crippen/ (accessed February 2019)

34. Francisco, Don. "Marriage and Divorce Myth 2 - Is Divorce a Sin?" Rocky Mountain Ministries.

35. Hunt, June. "How to Respond to Verbal and Emotional Abusers" The Christian Post. http://www.christianpost.com/news/how-to-respond-to-verbal-emotional-abusers-78253/ (accessed February 2019).

36. Cunningham, Alison, Linda Baker. "Little Eyes, Little Ears: How Violence against a Mother Shapes Children as They Grow" London Family Court Clinic. https://www.canada.ca/content/dam/phac-aspc/migration/phac-aspc/sfv-avf/sources/fem/fem-2007-lele-pypo/pdf/fem-2007-lele-pypo-eng.pdf (accessed February 2019)

37. Cunningham, Alison, Linda Baker. "Little Eyes, Little Ears: How Violence against a Mother Shapes Children as They Grow" London Family Court Clinic. https://www.canada.ca/content/

dam/phac-aspc/migration/phac-aspc/sfv-avf/sources/fem/fem-2007-lele-pypo/pdf/fem-2007-lele-pypo-eng.pdf (accessed February 2019)

38. Holcomb, Lindsey, Justin Holcomb. *Is It My Fault: Hope and Healing for Those Suffering Domestic Violence.* Chicago: Moody Publishers, 2014.

39. Fortune, Marie. *Keeping the Faith: Guidance for Christian Women Facing Abuse.* San Francisco: Harper One, 1995.

40. Crippen, Jeff. "Dealing With the Abuser" Sermon Audio.

41. Fortune, Marie. *Keeping the Faith: Guidance for Christian Women Facing Abuse.* San Francisco: Harper One, 1995.

42. Heggen, Carolyn. *Sexual Abuse in Christian Homes and Churches.* Eugene: Wipf and Stock, 2006.

43. Crippen, Jeff. *A Cry for Justice: How the Evil of Domestic Abuse Hides in Your Church.* Calvary Press, 2012.

44. Kroeger, Catherine. Quote in book *Domestic Violence: What Every Pastor Needs to Know* by Al Miles. Minneapolis: Fortress Press, 2011.

45. Crippen, Jeff. "'Christian' Enabling of the Abuser Increases His Attacks on the Victim" A Cry for Justice. http://cryingoutforjustice.com/2015/11/30/christian-enabling-of-the-abuser-increases-his-attacks-on-the-victim/ (accessed February 2019)

46. Moore, Russell. "The Church and Violence Against Women" Russell Moore. http://www.russellmoore.com/2014/09/09/the-church-and-violence-against-women/ (accessed February 2019).

47. Adams, Carol. "When the Abuser Is Among Us: One Church's Response to a Perpetrator" Faith Trust Institute. http://www.faithtrustinstitute.org/resources/articles/When-the-Abuser-Is-Among-Us.pdf (accessed February 2019)

48. Crippen, Jeff. *A Cry for Justice: How the Evil of Domestic Abuse Hides in Your Church.* Calvary Press, 2012.

49. Roberts, Barbara. "The Bible DOES allow divorce for domestic abuse" A Cry for Justice. http://cryingoutforjustice.com/2014/10/10/the-bible-does-allow-divorce-for-domestic-abuse/ (accessed February 2019)

50. The Mama Bear Effect. "Putting Child Safety First"

51. Bancroft, Lundy. "Understanding and Breaking Free From Relationship Violence – Chat Transcript" Pandora's Project. http://www.pandys.org/lundybancroft-transcript.html (accessed February 2019)

52. Vernick, Leslie. "Can I Divorce My Abusive Spouse?" Leslie Vernick. http://leslievernick.com/can-i-divorce-my-abusive-spouse/ (accessed February 2019)

53. Bancroft, Lundy. "Understanding and Breaking Free From Relationship Violence - Chat Transcript" Pandora's Project. http://www.pandys.org/lundybancroft-transcript.html (accessed February 2019)

54. Bancroft, Lundy. "Understanding and Breaking Free From Relationship Violence - Chat Transcript" Pandora's Project. http://www.pandys.org/lundybancroft-transcript.html (accessed February 2019)

55. Crippen, Jeff. "No Abuser is Hidden From His Sight" Sermon Audio.

56. Women's Resource Service. "Grief and Loss after Abuse"

57. Fortune, Marie. *Keeping the Faith: Questions and Answers for the Abused Woman.* New York: Harper Collins, 1987.

About the Author

Robin Mullins Senger is a writer, speaker and advocate for faith-based victims of domestic violence and spiritual abuse. She is also the founder and Executive Director of *God Hates Abuse Project,* a non-profit organization committed to removing religious misconceptions that prevent women, men and children from living fulfilling lives free from abuse. For more information, visit www.godhatesabuse.org or email her at robin@godhatesabuse.org.

Robin is also a Toxic Relationship Resiliency Life Coach. Her company, *Butterfoot Life Coaching,* empowers survivors of an abusive relationship to recognize their value and potential, identify their goals, and move toward their dreams. Survivors create a meaningful life and thrive instead of staying stuck in survival mode.

Raised in the Oregon Outback, she now enjoys living and recreating with her family in the Colorado Rockies. You can also connect with her on Facebook: https://www.facebook.com/godhatesabuse/

www.ingramcontent.com/pod-product-compliance
Lightning Source LLC
Chambersburg PA
CBHW050301010526
44108CB00040B/1957